SUCCESSFUL PLANTERS

Georgia Orcutt

Structures Publishing Co. 1977
Farmington, Mich. 48024

Editor: Shirley M. Horowitz

Cover photo, Hedrich-Blessing, Chicago

ISBN: 0-912336-48-X(cl.)
ISBN: 0-912336-49-8(pa.)
L.C.: 77-86465

Current printing (last digit)
10 9 8 7 6 5 4 3 2 1

Structures Publishing Co.
Box 423, Farmington, Mich. 48024

Contents

1
Planters and the Home Environment

Superstitions about green thumbs aside, anyone can garden successfully with planters as long as he or she uses common sense. You cannot expect a tree or a shrub to flourish if it is simply shoved into a wooden box and forgotten. If a plant is to thrive in a container, it must have the same elements it would require in the wild: light, food, moisture, and room to grow. Since a poorly positioned or improperly built structure can affect a plant's environment, you must consider several basic factors before building or planting.

DRAINAGE

Inadequate drainage frequently causes problems in planter gardening. A planter that functions correctly allows moisture to be held by the plant's root system long enough to provide sustenance, but no longer! If soil becomes waterlogged, plant roots will decay rapidly and rot.

The best system to assure adequate drainage uses a series of holes in the bottom. Planters with only one central opening can also work well, but be careful that the hole does not become clogged with dirt; the best way to keep it open is to cover it with a concave piece of broken clay pottery.

If your planter does not allow for drainage openings (if it is made of concrete or other material that cannot be drilled through), try lining the bottom with several inches of stone and placing one or more individual pots, which do have drainage holes, inside it.

Fill the planter with stones until the individual pots are camouflaged. Use these inside pots as containers for your plants. Water applied directly to the stones soaks into the plant's roots through the bottom of the planters. If you use a single pot to hold a large plant, be sure to allow room between its walls and those of the planter so that you can easily pull the pot out to transplant or move the plant.

Checking for Adequate Drainage

There are several ways to check for adequate drainage. A planter is not functioning correctly if water pools on the top or streams out the bottom just minutes after watering. Ideally, you will notice moisture around the base of a planter, and if the container directly touches a base of cement or wood, a moisture mark should appear on the surface beneath and around it. Even cement planters show signs of "sweating." Consider this fact if your planter stands in the house, or on a patio. Concrete blocks and cement floors can become stained in just a few weeks, often permanently. Avoid unsightly discolored rings by placing saucers and trays under your planters. A nonporous material such as plastic works well. If you prefer to use clay or wood, first paint it on the inside with several layers of enamel.

Improving Drainage

By keeping a planter off the ground, by as little as an inch, you can also improve its drainage. And, where planters are used in grassy areas, keeping them raised discourages infestation by burrowing insects.

Wooden runners, blocks, feet and short legs successfully elevate planters. But remember to do this *before* you add the soil! Even a small container becomes surprisingly heavy when filled.

SOIL MIX

Many different kinds of soil are suitable for use in planters—even the topsoil out of your own backyard provided you add enough organic material to make it fertile, with air spaces so your plant's roots will not smother.

Ways to Provide Proper Drainage—*Insufficient drainage, one of the most common problems in planter gardening, can easily be prevented. (a) A planter with an opening in the bottom is used inside a larger planter without such an opening. Gravel forms a bottom layer into which excess water can drain. (b) A broken piece of clay pottery is placed over a single drainage opening to keep it from becoming clogged with soil. A small piece of screen works equally well. (c) A layer of gravel on the bottom of a planter with a single opening keeps the hole from becoming clogged. A similar layer on the top of the soil adds a decorative touch, and helps retain moisture in the soil. (d) A tray without drainage openings is lined with gravel and used to hold several smaller individual planters that do have openings. (e) A base in a large planter box is constructed with openings between the bottomboards; water will drain out between the spaces. (f) A large cube planter contains numerous openings in the bottom, so water will drain out evenly.*

Healthy plants require a porous soil that drains well. Soil that contains a high percentage of clay is one of the worst to use in a planter, since it becomes soggy and traps water. Your plants depend on their soil for moisture regulation and nutrition, so spend some time figuring out the ingredients that best suit their needs.

If you want to use several planters in your home or yard, mix various ingredients and make your own economical soil compounds. If you do not have the time or the room to do this, or if you are only interested in filling one small container with soil, select a prepackaged brand from a garden supply store.

Types Available

The following materials form some basic soil mix components, all widely available at stores that sell soils and plant products.

Individual small planters are attractively grouped in multi-shelved decorator planter, on beds of small stones. Water applied directly to the stones is taken up through the plants' root systems. (Earthway Products Inc.)

Waterproof plastic plant mat protects floors or tables from moisture marks. Raised veins channel water, and rim prevents overflow. (Lillian Vernon photo)

Sphagnum Peat Moss: An organic compound, peat is composed of partially decayed, dried vegetable matter. Substitutes for peat that serve basically the same function include sawdust and ground tree bark.

Vermiculite: This sterile material, shaped into tiny cubes, contains potassium and magnesium; it can

Keeping Planters Elevated—*By allowing space for air beneath planters, even as little as an inch in height, drainage can be improved and moisture marks eliminated. (a) A base mounted on wheels facilitates mobility and keeps planter off the ground at the same time. (b) Metal legs form a holder for many different kinds of planters, and keep them securely off the floor. (c) Inconspicuous wooden blocks keep planter raised a safe distance. (Stim-U-Plant Laboratories, Inc.)*

both retain moisture and release it. Vermiculite helps keep soil light and gives air space to root systems.

Perlite: Not unlike processed puffed cereals, perlite is volcanic material that has been expanded by heating. Serving the same function as vermiculite, perlite is preferred in rainy climates for outdoor planters, since it disintegrates slowly.

Sand: Sand is frequently used when making soil for large planters. Heavier than vermiculite or perlite, it provides essential minerals for any mix and its considerable weight makes a large planter more stable.

Fertilizer: Healthy plants require a balanced diet of nitrogen, phosphorus and potassium—the essential

Ways to Move Planters—*Planters of any size can be surprisingly heavy when filled with soil. (a) Casters attached to underside of planter allow it to be moved easily. (b) A hand truck, obtainable at a hardware store or available from a rental company, makes moving a large planter a reasonable task. (c) A series of wooden* *dowels, at least an inch in diameter, can be used to roll a large, filled planter a short distance. (d) A child's wagon turns moving into an easy task, as long as you have help getting the planter into it.*

nutrients. Fertilizer formulae refer to the quantities in which these three elements are present, always in the order given above. The percentages of 5-10-10 are the most widely applicable; this balance provides some nitrogen for leaf development, and higher amounts of the two other elements for flowering and root development. Limestone is also included in many mixes for its nutrient value.

Mix Your Own

For the following two basic mixes, measurements are given in terms of cubic feet, but adjust the relationships

Plastic rolling saucer with free-wheeling casters protects floors and carpets and lets you move heavy plants easily. (Lillian Vernon photo)

to your own system of measurement. Feel free to substitute equivalent ingredients from the preceding list of components. Keep in mind that a mix should basically be part organic material (peat, sawdust) and part mineral (vermiculite, fertilizer, limestone).

BASIC MIXES

For Houseplant Containers and Pots

1 cubic foot peat moss
1 cubic foot vermiculite
1/2 pound limestone
1/2 pound fertilizer

For Large Trees or Shrubs

1 cubic foot sand
2 cubic feet peat moss
1/2 pound fertilizer
1 pound limestone

Dampen the ingredients as you mix them together, in much the same way as you would make cement. Use a shovel or hoe and work slowly, but methodically. If you do not own a large tub for mixing, spread a plastic sheet on the ground and combine the ingredients there. Store excess soil in garbage cans or plastic pails or bags. *Further Information:* To obtain additional details on soil mixes suited to large planters, send 25¢ and a request for a copy of Bulletin #43 to: Department of Communication Arts, Publications Mailing Room, Cornell University, Research Park, Ithaca, NY 14853.

MOBILITY AND SIZE

Do not fill your planter until you have decided where to put it. If you are installing a large-scale planter, you have probably figured this out. But time and time again, eager gardeners position a planter in one place and a year later decide to move it, only to find it virtually immobile.

The reasons for relocating often involve more than a sudden change of mind. If the garden is continually expanding, you might want to move some planters aside to make room for others. Or, you might decide to redo the entire area as a season's project. Possibly you would like to be able to move flowering trees into the background when they have ceased to bloom, yet make them a prominent feature when they reach their peak. Maybe a tree planted in your yard or that of a neighbor has grown taller than you had anticipated, suddenly providing unwelcome shade for a planter that originally received full sun.

So, except when planters are permanently installed, they should possess the greatest degree of mobility possible, especially those with smaller outside potted plants and trees that you might want to move indoors in the winter.

Mounting planters on casters, runners or wheels offers one solution to mobility problems. If you are building a planter or making one out of a barrel or tub, design a base piece to fit around the bottom and hide the wheels from sight. Or, design a planter that can be taken apart with minimal work: use screws instead of nails to attach the sides, or build sides that slide up along tracks, working in much the same way as a window. A planter that can be taken apart is invaluable when you come to transplanting or moving the plants within it. Realize that planters, unlike flower pots, can be difficult to hold onto and that their weight when filled should not be taken lightly!

Common sense should tell you that the larger your plant, the larger the container required. Your plants can grow for at least one year, often longer, without being transplanted. Many varieties respond well if they are continually pruned at the roots to remain in a given space; others need larger quarters once their roots fill the planter.

Let the shape of the planter complement the shape of the plant growing in it as much as possible. A short, full and bushy plant usually looks best in a square or round planter of equal proportion. The shape of a taller tree or shrub should be accented by the planter, but not overwhelmed by it. Never let the planter take center stage over its plant, but allow room for root growth. To

Symmetry of Plants and Planters—*Plants and planters match gracefully, never competing against one another for attention. Note the balance and support provided by these planters.*

be safe, provide a minimum of six to ten inches of soil beneath the plant's roots. Some root systems demand much greater space than you might expect, and other plants may have a more rapid growth cycle than you anticipate. You can inquire at your local nursery or greenhouse about the space requirements of specific plants and trees.

2
Inside Planters: Locations and Needs

If a planter is to become part of the interior decor of your home, spend some time considering the factors that play an important part in a plant's success. Planters can enhance any room in your house, as long as they display healthy growing plants.

LIGHT

Using Available Light

The location of a planter with respect to sunlight and windows becomes a critical consideration. If you are going to rely on available light, be sure to purchase plants or trees suited to the exposures of your room. (See Chapter 9 for requirements of specific plants.)

Determine what directions your light comes from before selecting your plants. Stand with a compass in your hand or get your bearings from other landmarks in your neighborhood. The height, size and number of your windows determine how much light your rooms receive and how far into the room the light reaches. Here are some basic characteristics of the four exposures:

North: Windows that receive northern light are favorites with painters and artists, since they provide long hours of "crisp" but indirect light, especially in the winter. These windows admit few shadows, and let in enough light for many types of plants.
South: A window that faces directly south receives bright sunlight for a good part of the day, both morning and afternoon. Not all plants can tolerate this much sun, and may be burned by it. Geraniums, cacti and fruit trees are good choices for southern exposures.
East: Eastern exposures generally receive good morning sun and are suited to plants that need some

light, but not direct sun. Windows facing east throw shadows in the afternoon.
West: Many plants that thrive in eastern light also do well in western exposures, which provide afternoon light.

Many different kinds of plants thrive in the soft, indirect light of an eastern-facing window. (Chris Maynard photo)

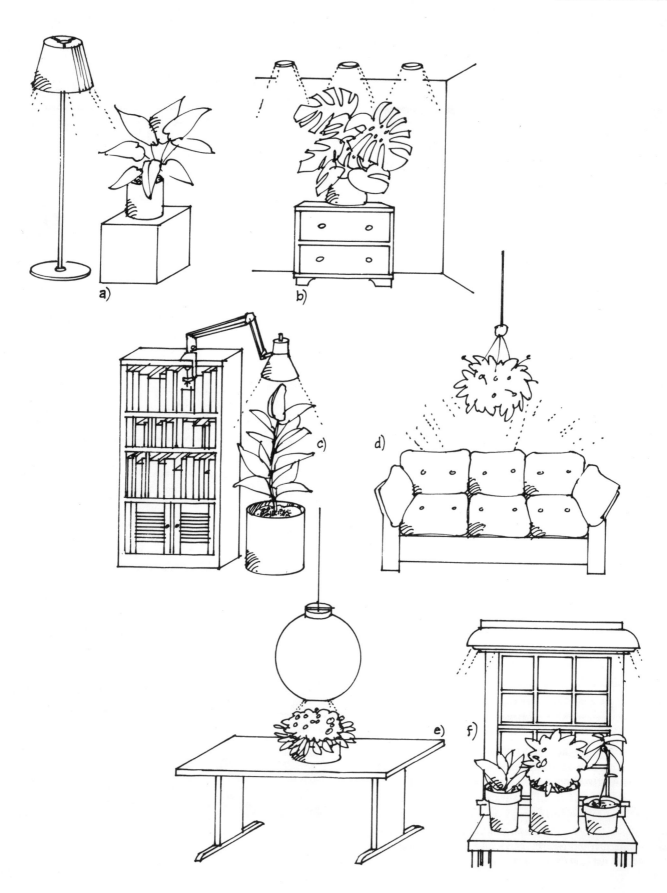

Because it receives no direct light from a window, this planter is positioned to take advantage of light from an ordinary floor lamp, no more than two feet away. (New York State College of Agriculture and Life Sciences at Cornell University)

Ways to Use Artificial Light with Planters—*(a) A standard household lamp with a 60 or 75 watt bulb provides enough light to maintain the needs of several plants that do not require direct sunlight. (b) Indirect lights mounted in the ceiling give off adequate light for many kinds of large-leaved plants. (c) A clamp-on or screw-on light fixture that can hold a standard household bulb or a special grow-light forms a versatile supplement to a plant's needs. (d) A hanging plant located just above a living room couch receives a boost of light from a fixture hidden behind the couch, shining up toward the plant. (e) An overhead fixture on an adjustable cord can be lowered to supply a table-top plant with adequate light. (f) A fixture mounted over a window supplies extra hours of light to plants that may not thrive in limited available light.*

A few hours of good light meet the needs of most plants. Your windows may receive light from a northeast or southwest direction and thus meet the requirements of many different plants. Experiment and use your eyes to discern the best places in your house for a planter.

The Plant Test

If you can wait a month or two before installing a large planter based on what you think will work, try a simple test. Stop at a local greenhouse and select a plant you would like to try in a planter, but buy a young one that will fit into an 8- or 10-inch clay pot. (Most large scale plants are sold in small sizes as well.) Place the pot on a box, or even on the floor with a saucer under it, and see if it thrives in the location chosen. Within a few weeks you will know if you have made the right choice, and you can more assuredly move on to a greater investment.

Using Artificial Lights

Artificial lights offer considerably more latitude for putting planters anywhere you choose. They also serve as good supplemental light for plants that need an extra boost. Unlike the sun, electricity has the potential to light an area 24 hours a day, and offers a steady and reliable energy source. Consider the different kinds of lights, and ways to use them with your planters.

Incandescent Lights: Standard household light bulbs are incandescent. They give off considerable heat and, although cheaper to buy than any other kind of house lighting, they cost more to operate. For tall planters, incandescent floodlights and spotlights mounted in the ceiling or on the floor (to shine upward) are frequently used. A lamp with a standard 60 or 75 watt bulb provides enough light to maintain the needs of several plants which do not require direct sunlight. Keep incandescent lights at least two feet away from your plants to avoid drying them out and burning their leaves.

Fluorescent Lights: As people who have grown plants in offices and school rooms know, fluorescent lights can have a positive influence on whatever grows within their range. Tube lights come in lengths varying from 18 inches to several feet, and are made in cool-white or warm-white colors. Since cool-white fluorescents release considerable amounts of blue light rays, they cre-

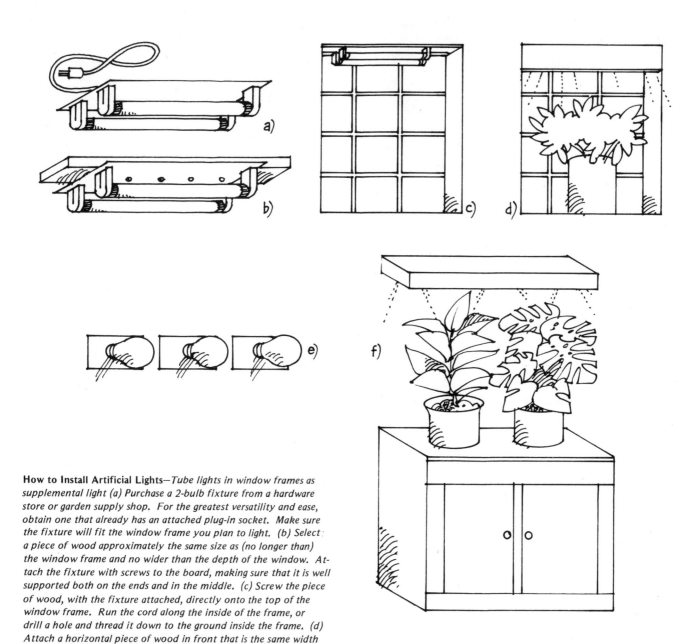

How to Install Artificial Lights—*Tube lights in window frames as supplemental light (a) Purchase a 2-bulb fixture from a hardware store or garden supply shop. For the greatest versatility and ease, obtain one that already has an attached plug-in socket. Make sure the fixture will fit the window frame you plan to light. (b) Select a piece of wood approximately the same size as (no longer than) the window frame and no wider than the depth of the window. Attach the fixture with screws to the board, making sure that it is well supported both on the ends and in the middle. (c) Screw the piece of wood, with the fixture attached, directly onto the top of the window frame. Run the cord along the inside of the frame, or drill a hole and thread it down to the ground inside the frame. (d) Attach a horizontal piece of wood in front that is the same width as the frame and the same depth as the total fixture, to conceal the tubes and to avoid glare from them. Bulbs for indirect light (e) Decide where in your home you'd like to provide some additional light. Ask an electrician to wire several socket boxes above this area. (f) Disguise the fixtures by running pieces of wood around the three sides—let the horizontal front piece of wood be deep enough to disguise the bulbs and eliminate glare.*

ate a cold, institutional feeling in a room. If possible, avoid this by using a combination of tubes, one cool-white and one warm-white, as the warm-white contains more red. Attach lights to the insides of bookcases, above windows, or use them directly above your planters. Fluorescents can be as close as eight inches to your plant, but they should be no further away than three or four feet for maximum effect.

FLUORESCENT LIGHT INSTALLATION

Fluorescent lighting may be easily installed above growing areas if a fixture box is conveniently located. You should have a rough idea of where you will want the fixtures; the box should be placed accordingly. Even if you do not initially expect to install auxiliary lighting, a pre-installed box with available wiring connections will make an eventual lighting hookup much easier.

If a box is intended for immediate or eventual use with a fluorescent fixture, select a box with a threaded center stud, since most fluorescent housings are designed to be affixed to the box by means of a locknut fastened over this stud.

Installation is simple. After following the manufacturer's instructions for the assembly of the fluorescent fixture, position it over the box and pull the connecting wires through. Splice and cap the wires (white-to-white, black-to-black), and secure the fixture onto the box stud. Switching, if not remotely controlled by previous breaking of current flowing to the box, will be self-contained in the fluorescent unit by means of a button or chain.

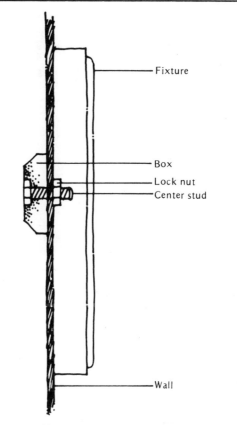

Fluorescent fixtures usually connect to electrical boxes by means of a lock nut fitting over a center stud in the box.

Here are two ways in which suspended, self-contained fluorescent fixtures can be mounted.

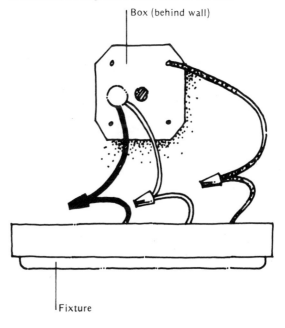

When installing fluorescents or any other light fixture, connect white to white and black to black wires—and be sure the current is shut off.

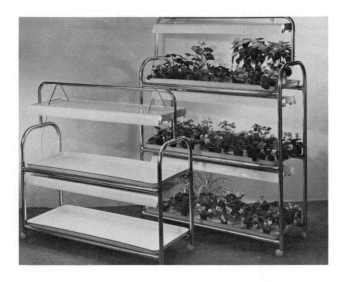

Carts with attached lighting fixtures come in many sizes with varying numbers of shelves. They provide efficient artificial light in the home. (Tube Craft, Inc.)

Grow-Lights: Lights made specifically for indoor gardening are available in garden shops. They combine essential amounts of red and blue light in one tube. Although more expensive than standard fluorescents, they give off less glare. Available in various lengths as tubes, or as bulbs, they can be used interchangeably in home lighting fixtures. Commercial trade brands include Agro-Lite and Gro-Lux.

Be sure with artificial light that your plants receive a minimum of 14 hours every day. Establish a schedule for turning the lights on and off—perhaps on after supper, off after breakfast—or attach an electric timing device so that the plants are never shortchanged.

TEMPERATURE

Most plants grow well in temperatures of 65 to 72 degrees, the normal range for heating a home in the winter. (During the summer, heat should not be a consideration as long as you are on the watch for dryness caused by poor ventilation.) Consider the way your home is heated and make necessary adjustments to establish the best location and climate for your planter.

Effects of Heating Systems

Forced Hot Water: Systems with baseboard radiation provide even heat, take up minimal floor space, and offer great flexibility in installing a planter. You can build above such heating units with little consequence. Planters made of metal or other synthetics can touch metal baseboards without conducting heat.

Forced Hot Air: A dry system that usually demands a humidifier or vaporizer to keep plants from becoming too dry, forced hot air takes up very little floor space and leaves many options for planter locations. It tends to provide heat in sudden bursts, which means that drafts occur. Keep planters away from registers so you do not block the heat, and watch for the amount of dust in the air. This system necessitates frequent washing of your plants' leaves.

Steam: Radiators can be extremely hot, so keep your plants' leaves away from them. Since they are large units, they often compete with planters for floor space. If allowed to touch a hot radiator over a period of time, ceramic planters can become stained and cracked from the heat. You can build a cabinet over a radiator, using a panel front that will let the heat through, and put planters on top of it. A wooden board at least a half-inch thick can be used on top of a radiator to hold a narrow planter, but frequent waterings are necessary when the heat is on. During the summer, use radiators as shelves for planter boxes full of greenery.

Electric: The best system for even heating and space economy, electric heat is also the most expensive. Since it provides heat from the floor upward, a planter can be located anywhere in the room.

Humidity

Remember that dry heat makes a plant sweat through its leaves and lose moisture rapidly. Simple watering does not combat this problem. Keep a humidifier or vaporizer running nearby (within two feet unless it is part of your heating system) for at least four hours per day. Frequent misting is also helpful. Or, place a pan of water under or next to your planter to help keep the air moist.

IDEAS FOR HOME USE AND INSTALLATION

Once you have surveyed your rooms and considered the amount of available light, the possibility of getting help from artificial light, and the location of your heating units, decide where your planters will be most effective.

Planters under and along stairway hide bareness and make entry to second level more graceful. (American General Products, Inc.)

Hundreds of models of planters, with thousands of plants, present endless combinations for all tastes and budgets. Do not settle on something that does not fit your room, even if it pleases your eye.

Room Design

Rather than just occupy space, planters serve many design functions. Some possibilities are listed below.

Fill a Bare Wall: If you have a large wall that is unsuited to bookcases or other pieces of furniture, a planter or two can take away the emptiness. Use a three-foot-high tube planter with a large, leafy tree, or several two-foot planter boxes this type of plants. A trailing plant, in a wall-mounted planter, can be an exciting substitute for a painting.

Divide Living Spaces: A planter four or five feet long and several feet high, filled with greenery, can act as a sepa-

rating wall to divide a room into distinct areas. Consider planters for dramatic division of a kitchen or living room from a dining area. If you use planters mounted on wheels, relocate your "wall" from time to time to try different arrangements.

Enhance an Entrance: If your front door opens into a large room, one or two planters on either side of the entrance create the effect of a vestibule or a hallway.

Form Partial Walls: Planters serve as three-or-four-foot walls in rooms where you may not want to block off all your open space. If you put a couch or a grouping of chairs in the center of a room, facing inward, a planter can hide the backs of your furniture pieces. It also can form separations in large rooms to give the illusion of several smaller rooms.

Round Out a Corner: In spacious rooms, corners pose problems in interior decorating. Try building a custom planter that just fits into a corner, or use a shape that takes up some room from an empty angled area.

Hide Stairways: A stairway that ascends abruptly from a living or dining room area leaves a number of steps exposed and unsightly. Fill in the space just below the stairs with a planter, or put one next to the staircase on the ground floor. A variety of hanging planters can also hide stairways.

Disguise an Unpleasant View: You may live where a window provides you with a view you would prefer not to see every day. To block a vista outside your window, but still let in some light, use a floor planter with a tall tree, or a hanging planter with long, trailing vines.

Hide Pipes: Some older houses have unsightly pipes running from floor to ceiling, which may require considerable expense to remove. A tall, cylindrical planter or a floor planter with a climbing vine can help. (Do not try to get a climbing vine to attach itself to a pipe that becomes hot. It won't work.)

Planters allow you to try many different room arrangements without going to the expense of redecorating the entire room. Moving the plants you are growing, or painting or covering a planter in a new way, may change the whole look of your home.

SPECIALTY HOME PLANTERS

A planter can also be used strictly for its ornamental appeal, providing the same kind of display as a piece of art. On a living room table, a bookcase shelf or a bedroom bureau, the following kinds of planters are eye catchers.

Bonsai gardening, an age-old Japanese art form, requires unique horticultural skills and presents specimens of dwarfed living trees, some hundreds of years old. In these two photographs, note the exquisitely simple planters that are used to echo and enhance the shapes of the trees growing in them. (Chris Maynard)

Bonsai Gardens

Bonsai is an age-old Japanese art that is becoming widely practiced in the United States today. It considers plants and their containers a means for creating a miniature environment that reflects the harmony of nature. A skilled hobby, bonsai uses woody plants (trees) that are painstakingly pruned, trained and cared for to grow as perfect miniatures, no more than a foot tall. The most sacred are 300 years old or more, and have been passed on through many generations of gardeners. Other commonly seen bonsai gardens feature trees at least 20 or 30 years old. Garden supply shops large enough to stock bonsai plants may offer specimens of this age.

In keeping with the meaning of bonsai, both plant and planter should be in perfect symmetry. Shallow trays, and simple but elegant clay dishes, function as planters in bonsai gardens.

To learn more about this fascinating form of container gardening, consult your local library or speak with other gardeners who are involved in bonsai. To find the group nearest you, write to the Nippon Bonsai Association, 608 North 21st Street, Montebello, California 90640.

Terrariums and Bottle Gardens

Garden shops across the country now sell supplies for terrarium gardens: special glass planters in all shapes and sizes, soil mixes, and fertilizer.

Select all the basics at such a store, or make your own garden from materials you have at home. Brandy snifters, large jars, and wine bottles can all be made into successful terrarium planters, as can a small fish bowl or a ten-gallon fish tank.

To plant the terrarium, be able to reach the bottom of the container you select: use one your hand will fit into, or one that has enough of a neck to admit a poking stick. Planters at least 18 inches high create the greatest effect.

Here is how to make a terrarium planter:

1. Cover the bottom of the container you have selected with small stones or gravel. If using a narrow-necked bottle, a small funnel or piece of paper rolled into a cone makes this step easier.

2. Add several inches of soil and even it out by shaking the container gently from side to side. Since you are creating a moist environment, use commercially prepared potting soil, rather than dirt that may contain

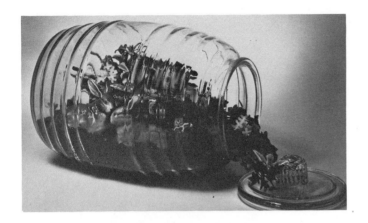

Planters for terrariums, available in many shapes and sizes, make dramatic conversational pieces and table top ornaments. (Riekes-Crisa Corp.)

other bacteria and plant spores. Foreign substances multiply and decay, spoiling the appearance of a terrarium.

3. Select plants several inches tall (see Chapter IX for suggestions) that will not be cramped in the space your container allows. Shake off the soil around their roots and push them into the terrarium's soil. Use your fingers if you can reach in; otherwise, use a ruler or narrow stick.

4. Add enough water to moisten the soil, but not to waterlog it.

5. For rectangular planters put on a tightly fitting top, made from pieces of glass or plexiglass cut to order at hardware stores. Pieces of plastic wrap secured with a rubber band also work, although not as attractive for permanent use. Corks or screw tops suffice on narrow bottles and jars.

6. Put your newly planted terrarium in a shady place for several days to let its plants become acclimated to their new environment. Check the planter from time to time and watch for any moisture on the sides. If condensation occurs, your system has too much water. Remove the cover for 24 hours and then seal your planter again. Repeat this process, if necessary, until the clouding ceases.

Display the planter where it will receive good light but not direct sun. If functioning properly, it acts as a miniature ecosystem, and requires virtually no care. As the plants grow larger, either move them to a more spacious planter or take them out of the terrarium for display elsewhere.

Living Centerpieces

Planters also serve as table ornaments or centerpieces. In place of cut flowers that survive for only a few days, consider a small planter full of living plants.

Tailor it to complement your table setting, and not to overshadow it. Use small glass bowls or china dishes with potted plants set into them. Line the bottom with pebbles and select delicate plants that are just a few inches high, so they will not block anyone's view across the table. Herbs are a good choice: they can create a lovely fragrance; if you wish, put one small plant at each place.

There is no reason why a centerpiece planter must always remain on the table. Make a temporary planter as a centerpiece only for the duration of your meal, and then return it to its regular growing spot.

3

Indoor and Outdoor Planters for City Gardeners

Growing plants add both color and life to a city apartment. But do not stop short after setting a pot of ivy on your windowsill! Planter gardening offers delightful options, even to those with limited growing space—possibilities range from a dozen flowering plants to an 11-foot tree. As long as the containers you select provide the basic requirements for plant growth, you can enjoy the rewards of gardening indoors, whether your domain is two rooms or twenty.

PRIMARY CONSIDERATIONS

Plant Needs

Take a critical look at your living room, kitchen and hallways. Are there places where the addition of a planter or two could highlight a nondescript area, or create a special effect? Evaluate the sources of available light in these areas. If you have just one window, perhaps in your living room, determine what direction it faces and how large an area in your room it lights. If you live in an older building with long windows set two feet above the floor, or if you have windows across from each other on opposite sides of a room, you can successfully position a planter as far away from a window as six or seven feet. Each room is different, and each window lets in varying degrees of light. Proximity of other buildings, time of day, and changing seasons all have an effect on available light. Don't always feel it necessary to set planters within inches of your windows; experiment with other areas that seem to you to receive adequate light.

In an apartment, you must live with what you have. Few people want to spend their own time and money installing new windows and skylights. So make the most out of what is there.

Walls that are painted white, rather than a dark color, help reflect available light. Some gardeners also feel that mirrors boost the amount of light that comes into a room. Whether mirrors can be proven to do this or not, they can dramatically show off a planter in smaller rooms.

Rather than hang curtains to give privacy to your living quarters, consider venetian blinds or bamboo shades that can be adjusted to admit some light, even when partially drawn. The leafy branches of a large tree against a window can function as curtains by offering privacy, while at the same time brightening the room by letting in some light.

If you have small children or pets in your household, keep planters out of the mainstream of traffic. A dog's wagging tail or a child's long-handled toy competing for space with a growing plant usually means disaster for the plant.

Using Inside Space Creatively

Since space is at a premium in most apartments and city homes, planters that serve dual purposes or fit into unused places deserve initial consideration. Some functional planters include the following:

Shelf Planters: Many styles of planters have room to store magazines and books (or what have you) on a small shelf or rack, and a place at the top for a sizable plant. Available in wood, plastic or metal, with and without legs, some fit into colonial motifs, while others are very modern. Although most shelf planters are 36 inches tall or taller, they usually occupy not more than one or two square feet of floor space.

Coffee Table Planters: There are many ways to enjoy the convenience of a coffee table that also functions as a planter. Purchase planter tables made out of

None of the planters shown in this photo are directly in front of windows, but all are positioned to receive adequate natural light. (Photo by the makers of Armstrong interior furnishings)

End table and bookshelf hold planters in room with limited space. Possibilities for economizing on floor space in small rooms are endless. (Photo by the makers of Armstrong interior furnishings.)

Corner planter with legs provides room for two pots of ferns, without sacrificing valuable floor space. (Photo by the makers of Armstrong carpet.)

Portable shelf planter with tiers of artificial lights makes gardening possible in even the darkest part of a room. (Earthway Products, Inc.)

butcher block or other woods. Some outdoor furniture shops sell wrought iron tables designed to serve as planters, but these may not fit into your interior decor.

If you have an old, round wooden coffee table, you can simply cut a hole in the center, the size determined by a clay pot that will just fit. Or, you can use a space in the center of a table to hold a shallow tray full of pebbles with several containers on it. Attach a plastic box or build your own out of metal and fasten it to the underside of the table. The whole table can become a useful planter, a place for coffee cups and ashtrays, and also a conversation piece.

Bookcase Planters: Books and plants seem to go together. If you have a standing bookcase, leave the top free to hold a planter of comparable length and width. This might be a metal or plastic trough, or a box you have built yourself. Or, leave several shelves or portions of shelves free to hold pots full of trailing plants. You can also make a planter for the top of a bookcase that holds several large pots, but reveals them only from the rim up. The bottoms of the pots can be hidden by a horizontal piece of wood.

Planters with Artificial Lights: A boon to apartment gardeners are the various models of planters that include an electric light assembly. They contain plastic trays (you can substitute your own, made of wood or

glass) and a lighting fixture mounted overhead. Buy them as one unit, and use them wherever you have access to an electrical outlet. Some dramatic places to show them off include unused fireplaces (a great way to use a fireplace in the summer). They can also transform a kitchen counter into a fragrant and useful herb garden. Varying heights and widths are available, with one light or several. If you want to make a considerable investment, of $100 or more, you can purchase multi-shelf units that offer from 8 to 24 square feet of gardening space. Planters with artificial lights fit in corners, against walls, or even in closets that otherwise receive no light at all.

Ladder Planters: To make use of vertical space, several companies offer planters that are in effect miniature ladders. Some have holes cut in the tops or on the

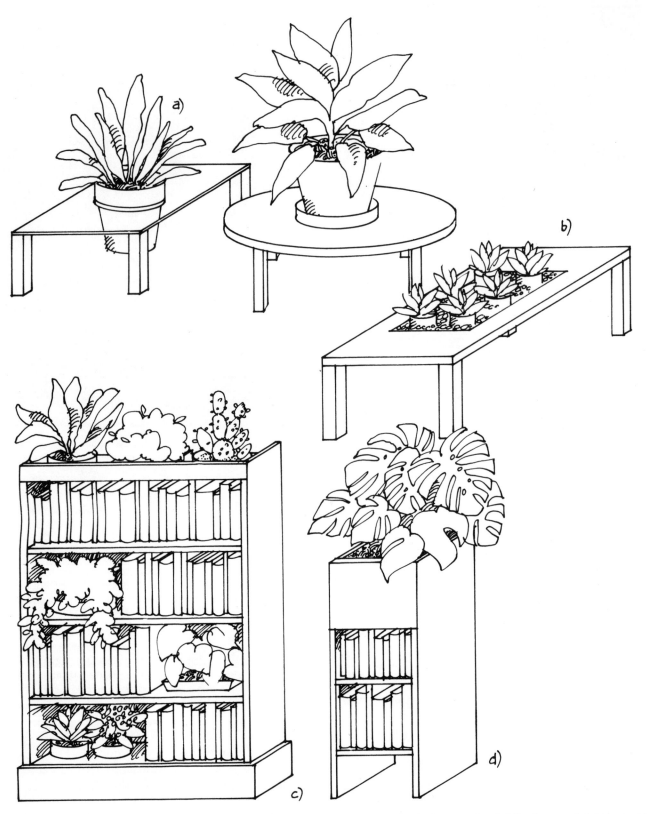

Using Space Creatively—*(a) Coffee table planter makes room for large-size pot in hole cut in center. (b) Rectangular coffee table planter is made by cutting a shape in the center, and recessing a tray to hold individual small planters. (c) Book shelves are natural places to save space with planters. Top shelf has been made into long, vertical planter, and individual pots are covered with a horizontal board. (d) Vertical planter provides room for books or records underneath plant.*

Collapsible light/shelf unit accommodates a variety of planters on a table. Such a device could also be used under cabinets, in closets, or even in fireplaces during the summer. (Westinghouse Electric Corp.)

steps to hold pots; others are designed with slatted "rungs." They come in redwood and other materials, including wrought iron and lucite. A standard wooden step ladder from a hardware store can also serve as a planter, and four-foot or six-foot sizes that have been painted or stained and filled with plants can be very effective.

Ways to use planters in confined spaces are endless. Let your imagination be your guide and shop around to discover those best suited to your needs.

HANGING PLANTERS

Suspending a planter from the ceiling or attaching it to a wall or some woodwork can save valuable floor space. Hundreds of models of hanging planters are sold commercially and, depending on your needs and your pocketbook, you can choose from many different materials.

Advantages and Disadvantages of Popular Materials

Plastic: Nurseries and greenhouses usually sell their hanging plants in plastic pots that have a convenient saucer attached at the bottom to catch any excess moisture after watering. These pots work perfectly well at home. Light in weight and sold individually in different styles, colors, and sizes, they usually come with wires attached for hanging.

Clay: Terra cotta planters for hanging also come in varying sizes, with or without drainage holes. The larger ones, up to 16 inches in diameter, generally

Portable, multi-shelf planter with built-in artificial lights can be used in a windowless room to provide an area for growing plants. (Westinghouse Electric Corp.)

are made with an attached saucer. But be careful. A hanging clay planter can be very heavy, and a hazard if not hung securely. To adequately support this heavy a planter, hooks should be attached to framing studs.
Metal: Some of the newer lightweight metals, including aluminum, make good hanging planters since they require relatively little weight support. Most are not built with drainage openings, so use another pot made of Styrofoam or plastic as a liner. Metal planters with shiny, mirrored finishes easily show finger marks and moisture spots. Clean them frequently with commercial window cleaner.
Redwood: A popular, weather-resistant planter material, redwood comes in hanging versions of the classic container so frequently seen on patios and balconies, holding small trees and shrubs.
Fabric: Because of their negligible weight, planters made from burlap and other fabrics are suited to hanging plants. It is a good idea to use another container inside such planters, both to keep water from dripping out the bottom and to give them shape.

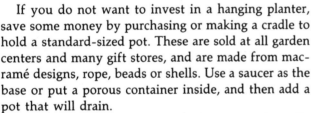

Two sizes of ladder planters, modeled after the conventional step ladder, provide extra inches of growing space without taking up extensive amounts of floor space. (Stim-U-Plant, Inc.)

This version of the ladder planter had ready-cut holes to secure planters from falling. (Heath Manufacturing Co.)

If you do not want to invest in a hanging planter, save some money by purchasing or making a cradle to hold a standard-sized pot. These are sold at all garden centers and many gift stores, and are made from macramé designs, rope, beads or shells. Use a saucer as the base or put a porous container inside, and then add a pot that will drain.

An essential part of a hanging planter is its base. Be sure it can hold water and will not drip on your floors or carpets each time you add water. (If the planter was not designed with this in mind, put a plate or saucer in the bottom, or line it with plastic or metal.) Do not cheat on the watering! Since warm air rises, be alert lest the soil dry out, especially in the winter when the heat is on. Start misting your plant the day you hang it, and give it at least two mistings per week thereafter. Buy one of the plastic spray bottles that are just for misting plants.

When filled with soil, a large planter becomes very heavy and unwieldy. A hanging planter 14 inches in diameter could weigh as much as 75 or 100 pounds. Make sure anything you hang is securely attached before you walk away and leave it alone. Toggle bolts or reinforced hangers offer the best support. Be sure hooks and other hanging devices make contact with studs or other support systems (see pp. 29–30).

Suspend hanging planters from chains, ropes, wire, strips of leather or thinly braided cords. Be sure that whatever you use is divided into equal lengths, so your planter hangs evenly.

Position a hanging planter to receive sufficient light, but keep it far enough away from windows and walls so the plant's branches and leaves touch nothing but air. Hanging plants seem to know when they are cramped, and will show it. Remind yourself to turn the planter from time to time so your plant grows evenly with respect to available light.

OUTDOOR CITY GARDENING

If you expand your city growing space to a balcony, patio or rooftop, you can try out many other styles of urban gardening. Planters enable you to develop growing room outdoors on a seasonal basis.

In the city you have two elements to contend with that rural gardeners do not face, at least to as large a degree—pollutants and grime are more concentrated and more visible in city air. They readily leave their marks as soot and grease, and threaten to hinder the health of whatever you grow. To combat their effects, mist and wash your plants frequently. If you do

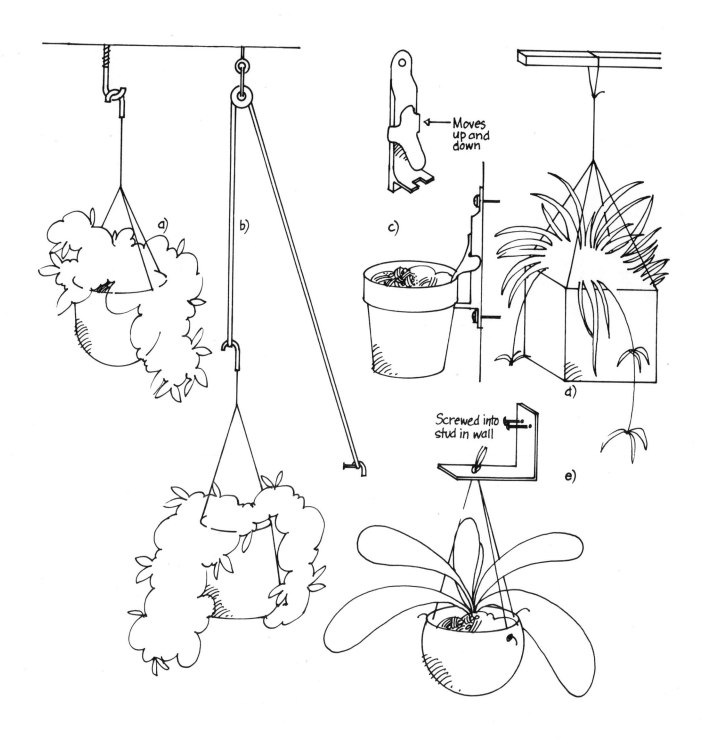

Attaching Hanging Planters—*Be sure hanging plants are well secured, since they can be a hazard if not well anchored. (a) Large metal hook with screw-in threads, available at any hardware store. Make sure you have contact with a stud or beam, and not simply with ceiling plaster or sheet rock. (b) A simple pulley, attached by an eye screwed into the ceiling, makes it possible to lower and raise heavy plants for watering and misting. (c) Clip-on pot holder comes in various sizes and is simply attached to wall or woodwork by means of two screws. The pot clips onto bottom part of hook, and sliding upper part can be adjusted to hold rim securely. (d) A simple but safe method for hanging a planter is by means of a rope that loops around a beam. (e) Fancy versions of plant hangers include L-hanger that screws into wall at one end and supports plant at right angle from other end. Such hangers are available in metal, wood and plastic.*

A simple but unique invention for hanging plants, this holder accommodates four individual pots and is ideal for patios or rooftops. (Skyhook)

A fabric planter is a new kind of hanging container, both light in weight and available in different styles. (Adam Jay, Inc.)

Classic redwood tubs are available in models suited to hanging. (Stim-U-Plant Laboratories, Inc.)

not have access to a hose and faucet, use large-size spray bottles filled with water.

Beware also of the heat that a city generates through the materials from which it has been built. Brick, concrete and asphalt reflect heat, and can turn a small garden area into a furnace. Burning noonday sun can wither a seedling in less than an hour. Line concrete patios or asphalt roofs with a material that will absorb some of the heat. Use pieces of black plastic strips or indoor-outdoor carpeting under planters. The straw matting sold by swimming pool supply shops as a slip-resistant surface for diving boards can also be used; it comes in handy rolls and tolerates rain well.

Awnings, shades and even inventions as primitive as an umbrella with strips cut into it, should also be considered as accessories to your planter garden for shielding your plants from burning sun.

Make spot checks throughout the day as the sun moves across the sky, to see what areas on a balcony or patio receive the most sun and which are shaded by adjacent buildings. For severe shading, mount planters on wheels or buy ready-made plant stands so you can move your planters out of the shade to follow the sun.

Plant Selection

You can raise many different kinds of plants in limited outdoor space. Seed companies, having realized the trend toward gardening in confined areas, offer many strains of dwarfed or miniature plants. From seeds, you can raise such popular annuals as marigolds, asters, dahlias and impatiens, which will provide color throughout the summer. If you live in a climate where the winters are severe, you might select plants that you can bring inside and keep going throughout the winter. Begonias, azaleas and coleus are favorites for their color and their hardiness indoors.

If you have neither the proper conditions nor the inclination to continue your gardening throughout the year, consider this when you select your plants. Do not tie up money in expensive trees or perennials that need special care after the summer, but that will have no place to spend the winter.

A large balcony that receives some sun, or a roof that is flat enough to walk on, can be ideal places for a planter garden. But if you have any doubts about the safety of a structure and how much weight it can hold, check with the local building inspector before you start planning. Several 5-gallon containers filled with soil, plus a barrel full of water to meet plant needs, could add 1,000 pounds of weight to an area. Be sure also to check with the landlord to ascertain that outdoor gardening or access to the roof is permitted.

However ambitious your designs for filling available growing space, remember to keep things simple and mobile in case you need to unbuild it one day and move it to another address.

RAISING VEGETABLES IN CONTAINERS

A recent explosion in urban gardening stems from the discovery that vegetables can be successfully grown in containers. Raising your own vegetables at home, whether as a hobby or as a reaction to supermarket inflation, or both, is a fascinating and rewarding pastime.

Greenhouses sell a variety of seedlings ready to start in gardens—tomatoes, cabbage and many kinds of herbs are generally available at even the smallest gar-

Pixie Hybrid tomatoes thrive in small planters, and make excellent patio or balcony plants. (W. Atlee Burpee Co.)

den centers. But, as is also true with flowering plants, there is no reason why a city gardener cannot start vegetable plants from seeds with success. Starting from seed also provides selection from a greater variety of plants. Reading seed catalogues is perhaps one of the most popular indoor hobbies for today's gardeners during winter months—admiring the glorious, colorful pages, learning the dos and don'ts of what is offered, and considering all the plants that are available in seed form. The urban gardener can enjoy seed catalogues as much as the truck farmer does! (For addresses of seed companies to write for catalogues, see the appendix.) Pay careful attention to the descriptions given in the catalogues and select varieties that are recommended for container propagation.

Some vegetable plants can tolerate shade, but others will be stunted and unproductive if they fail to receive adequate sunlight. Assume that plants which bear fruit above the ground—tomatoes, squash, cucumbers, etc. —will need more sunlight than those that do not. To obtain a brochure on how much shade or sun specific vegetables can handle and still flourish, write to the U.S. Department of Agriculture, Washington, DC and request a copy of *Home and Garden Bulletin # 163.*

After you have selected the seedlings or seeds you want to raise, decide on the containers you will grow

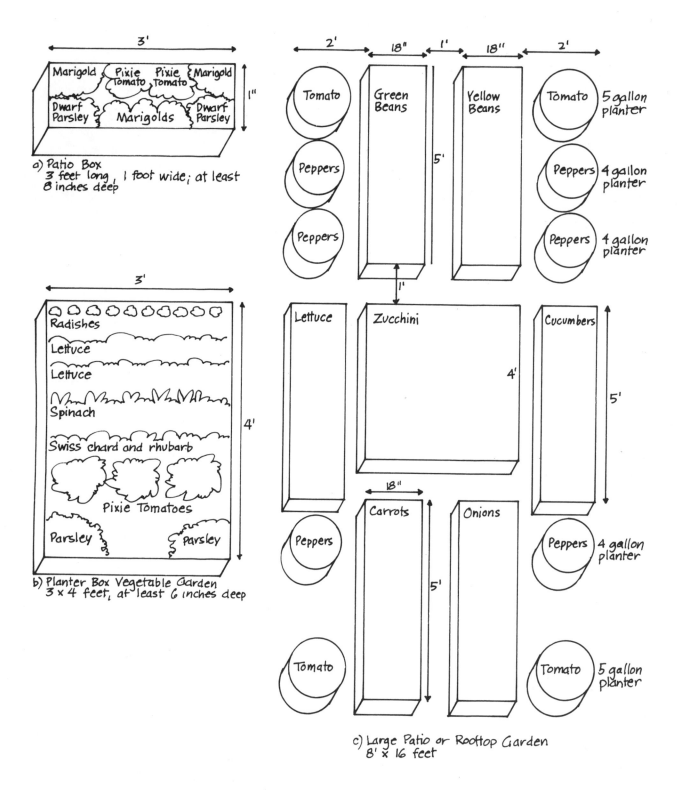

a) Patio Box
3 feet long, 1 foot wide; at least
8 inches deep

b) Planter Box Vegetable Garden
3 x 4 feet, at least 6 inches deep

c) Large Patio or Rooftop Garden
8' x 16 feet

Layouts for Patio, Balcony or Rooftop Gardens—*There are
hundreds of variations you can use to plan what you will grow
where in your garden plot. Here are just a few suggestions. The
first two are recommended by the W. Atlee Burpee Company.*

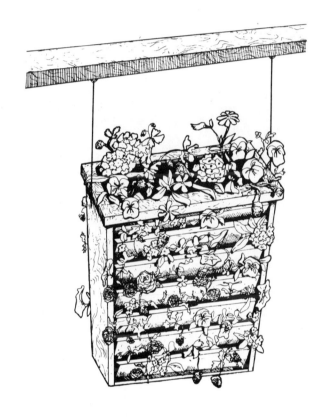

Three versions of two-sided vertical gardens for use on porches, patios, sundecks, and terraces. They also serve as excellent dividers, or as screens for privacy. (Michael Becker, Palo Alto, California)

them in. Both from a practical standpoint and to eliminate excess weight on balconies, patios, and rooftops, favor planters that are relatively light and steer away from materials such as brick, stone and concrete.

Suitable Materials

Wooden Boxes: If made of pine or another softwood, or from water resistant woods such as redwood, teak

How to Build a Simple Patio Planter Box—

Materials needed: 2 1 x 4 16 inch sides
                     2 1 x 4 10 inch ends
                     3 1 x 4 16 inch bottoms
                     Glue, nails, hammer

(a) Assemble 4 side pieces so that shorter ends are inside longer sides. (b) Drive nails partway into ends before making complete connections. (c) Use a thin bead of white glue for extra reinforcement along all jointed seam ends. (d) Drive nails through to final points. (e) Check square of angles before nailing on base. (f) Add base pieces, allowing a quarter inch of space between base boards for drainage. (g) Completed box is ready for coating of cuprinol or another preservative.

or cypress, simple boxes can be inexpensive and convenient planters. They are like miniature garden plots. You can make your own to the size you wish, or purchase them ready-made at garden supply stores. Wooden wine cases and wooden milk crates also make ideal box planters. Be sure to paint the inside with cuprinol, or another preservative to prevent rotting.

Plastic Tubs: Large plastic tubs in various colors, with or without saucers, are sold in many garden centers. Made of a nonporous material, they retain moisture longer than clay. A standard size 14 inches across holds five or six gallons of soil.

Wooden Tubs: The perennial favorites in wooden tubs are made of redwood and are available in many sizes, some with fancy metal bands on the outside. They resist moisture and last for many years.

Styrofoam Pots: Although lightweight and far less expensive than those made of some other materials, Styrofoam planters are susceptible to tipping over and being blown away by high winds. They make good liners for planters that do not have drainage holes. If anchored by bricks or heavy stones, Styrofoam food coolers make excellent planters.

Wicker and Straw Baskets: Almost any gift, department or even grocery store sells baskets of one kind or another. They make attractive planters if lined with heavy pots, such as those made of clay. Line bottoms with saucers to prevent mildew.

Wire Baskets: Since they frequently drip after watering, wire baskets are far more practical to use outdoors than in your home. Hang them, and line them with sphagnum moss to hold the soil. Garden supply shops sell many different sizes and shapes. You can also adapt other kinds of wire baskets; bicycle baskets work very nicely, and so do three-tiered vegetable baskets.

Trash Cans: A 15-gallon trash barrel or a 10-gallon drum makes a suitable planter, as long as the soil drains well and the plant's roots receive some water. Beware of the heat that metal can give off and, if possible, paint before using.

Clay Pots: Readily available in sizes up to 18 inches in diameter, just about anything grows outdoors in clay pots. Since they are porous, they will "sweat," and thus dry out quickly. Plan to water anything you grow in clay at least once a day.

How Large a Planter Do You Need?

The depth and width of your planters should meet the needs for root development of whatever you are

Vegetables to Raise in Planters: The vegetables listed below are some of the more easily grown planter crops. Study seed catalogues for additional suggestions and for details on thinning and spacing.

Vegetable	Required Soil Depth	Height at Maturity	Days to Maturity
Beans (snap)	10–12″	up to 2′	50–55
Beans (lima)	10–12″	up to 2′	65–75
Beans (pole)	10–14″	up to 8′ (require support)	80–90
Beets	12–14″	greens to 1′	55–60
Broccoli	8–10″	up to 16″	55–85
Cabbage (green)	8–10″	up to 10″	60–90
Cabbage (red)	8–10″	up to 8″	90–100
Cucumber	16–18″	up to 6′ if supported to climb	60–65
Dandelion	6–8″	up to 1′	85–95
Eggplant	16–18″	up to 3′	60–75
Herbs (in general)	6–8″	up to 3′	40–60
Lettuce (head)	4–6″	up to 10″	65–80
Lettuce (leaf)	2–4″	up to 8″	45–50
Onion	10–12″	up to 14″	95–120
Peas	10–12″	up to 4′ (require support)	60–70
Peppers	14–16″	up to 3′	60–75
Radish	6–8″		20–30
Spinach	6–8″	up to 8″	40–50
Squash (summer)	14–16″		50–60
Squash (winter)	16–18″		75–120
Tomatoes (cherry)	8–10″	up to 30″	60–70
Tomatoes	18–20″	up to 4′ (require support)	70–85

growing. As you might assume, you would be wasting valuable space to grow lettuce in a 50-gallon drum; and so, too, would you do injustice to a carrot plant by expecting it to thrive in a 5-inch pot.

There is no standard way to measure the capacity of the planters you use. Depending on the soil mix, one pound of soil could fit into several different-sized containers.

Look at your container in terms of its depth in inches, and translate this to the plants that are appropriate to grow in it. Consult the vegetable and flower charts above and on p. 37 for some suggestions on easily grown container plants and their soil requirements.

Saving Space Outdoors

If you feel you have enough time to launch into large-scale urban gardening that fills every inch of your space with growing plants, you might want to consider using vertical containers to get the most from your garden. A

Dramatic pyramid planter, complete with its own light, gracefully uses vertical space to save on ground area. (California Redwood Association)

Flowers to Raise in Planters: The flowers listed below include some of the more easily grown planter varieties. Consult seed catalogues for further details, and variations in days to maturity.

Flower	Required Soil Depth	Height at Maturity
Alyssum	6″	up to 9″
Celosia (dwarf)	6″	up to 11″
Coleus	6–8″	up to 15″
Geranium	8″	up to 15″
Impatiens	6″	6″ to 2′
Marigold	6–8″	up to 3′
Nasturtium	12″	1′
	(require support)	
Pansy	6″	up to 8″
Petunia	6″	up to 15″
Phlox	6″	7″
Zinnia (dwarf)	6″	6″

planter need not always be a box or a tub occupying horizontal space. In designing your city garden, let your imagination carry you away and lead you into experiments with other styles of planters. Here are a few to consider:

Vertical Walls: As long as the soil is well secured in a structure, plants will easily grow outward and upward. Living walls have been a part of limited-space gardening in European countries for centuries, and their design can be successfully imitated. Make your own vertical wall from wire mesh and pieces of wood, or purchase a planter that has been designed to provide vertical space. A wall that is 5 feet high and 6 feet long offers 30 more feet of garden room.

Pillar Planters: To take advantage of the vertical plane, but not to the extreme of using a wall, consider a pillar to serve the same function. Made from wire mesh and wood, pillars fill corners, or are hung above other planters.

Terraces: Also referred to as step gardens, terraces allow you to take advantage of several soil depths within a limited space. To save every inch of soil consider a terrace planter, which you can easily make from wood, for raising different crops in very limited space. A step planter three feet by five feet can contain varying levels of soil—6, 8, and 10 inches deep. Devote one row each to carrots, onions and lettuce and save yourself from using any extra pounds of soil.

Strawberry Planters: Some large seed companies and nurseries sell ready-made planters developed just for strawberries. Strawberry barrels are planters that come in heights up to 4 feet. They have 3-to-3-inch openings in alternating layers on all sides, and yield an entire summer's-worth of berries in very small space. The strawberry pyramid is another popular specialty planter, and one seed company boasts that with it, customers can "grow strawberries on a postage stamp."

Timing

Keep in mind that not all crops are ready to harvest at the same time. To keep your planters productive throughout the growing season, work out a schedule so plants are constantly growing, maturing and being harvested. A planter that in May is filled to the brim with crisp leaf lettuce can be ready for a late crop of snap beans to be planted in early June.

For Further Information: As gardening in planters becomes more popular, local and state agencies are turning their efforts toward the subject. Consult your nearby extension service and request a copy of their publications list, which will probably contain some literature pertaining to planter crops.

4

Window Planters

Turning part of your window into a planter offers both decorative and practical advantages. Window boxes, the most common form of window planters, open up many options for planter gardening. As basically immobile, attached planters, they have created magnificent seasonal displays in European countries for centuries, and many American homes have adopted the custom.

Outdoor window planters make it possible for you to grow a variety of flowering annuals. Seed companies have formulated new strains of flowering plants available in dwarf varieties—you get the same kind of flower from a dwarf plant as you would from a normal-sized plant, but the dwarf is narrower, shorter, and more compact. Dwarf varieties in your window box allow you to enjoy lovely colors without sacrificing your window view to plants that grow up past the windowsill.

Bulbs also frequently adorn window boxes; they come up year after year, or can be forced indoors for just one season's growth.

SELECTING A WINDOW PLANTER

Standard window boxes come in several materials and various sizes, starting from 18 inches in length and 4 inches in width. Look for them at garden supply shops and shops that sell pots and related items.

Materials

Metal: Aluminum, trough-shaped boxes, lightweight and durable, are usually painted in rustproof green or black. They are manufactured with or without drainage openings; those without openings should be used wherever you do not want excess water to drain out— for example, on a second floor or balcony that overlooks the street. Metal boxes are often used as liners for wooden window boxes.

Wood: A wooden window box, more versatile than metal, can be easily painted or stained to have a finished appearance. Redwood boxes abound. If you choose, you can build your own wooden planter box (see p. 42). Wooden boxes readily attach to various surfaces, since screws can be drilled through their sides.

Styrofoam: Best used as liners for other boxes, planter boxes made from Styrofoam are extremely lightweight, and can be knocked off balance with just a touch of the hand. They are also virtually impossible to install by themselves.

Fiberglass: Very lightweight, and also easy to keep clean, fiberglass window planter boxes serve as satisfactory liners or as actual planters. They should contain a layer of stones to provide additional weight. Most fiberglass boxes are made without drainage openings, so be on the watch for pooling water. Cut down on the amount of water you give to plants growing in such boxes, or drill openings in the bottom.

ATTACHING WINDOW PLANTERS

With little trouble, you can permanently attach a window box to the exterior sill of your house. But common sense should tell you to spend some time making it a compatible part of your decor.

Some manufacturers custom-design window planters to match the trim or the outside material, but this can be very expensive. A window box is not difficult to make and cover with siding, shingles, or clapboards, to complement the trim on your house. Liners and inside planter boxes are especially good; you can remove them at will and leave the installed planter intact.

A window planter can be attached to your exterior window area in several ways. A popular method uses right-angle brackets that fit the width of your planter

Fuchsias ornament a wooden window box and are also used in pro-fusion in planters arranged on the shingled exterior of this house. Window box is attached by means of wooden brackets, almost hidden from view by the plants' trailing branches. (Merry Gardens, Camden, Maine)

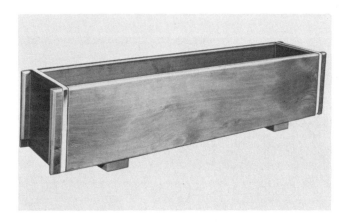

Redwood planter boxes come in various lengths and in varying finishes. This one features metal-reinforced ends. (Heath Manu-facturing Co.)

Wooden planter boxes range from the very plain to the very fancy. This modern version has a striking contemporary design. (Cali-fornia Redwood Association)

box. The supporting part of the bracket should extend at least two inches beyond the center point of your planter. If your house is made of wood, screw two pieces of wood, cut to fit the length of the bracket, directly to the exterior wall. Then screw on the bracket.

(See p. 40.) This method also works for houses made of brick, but you must use special masonry screws to pen-etrate the brick. Be sure you paint any wood used with preservative treatments to prevent rotting.

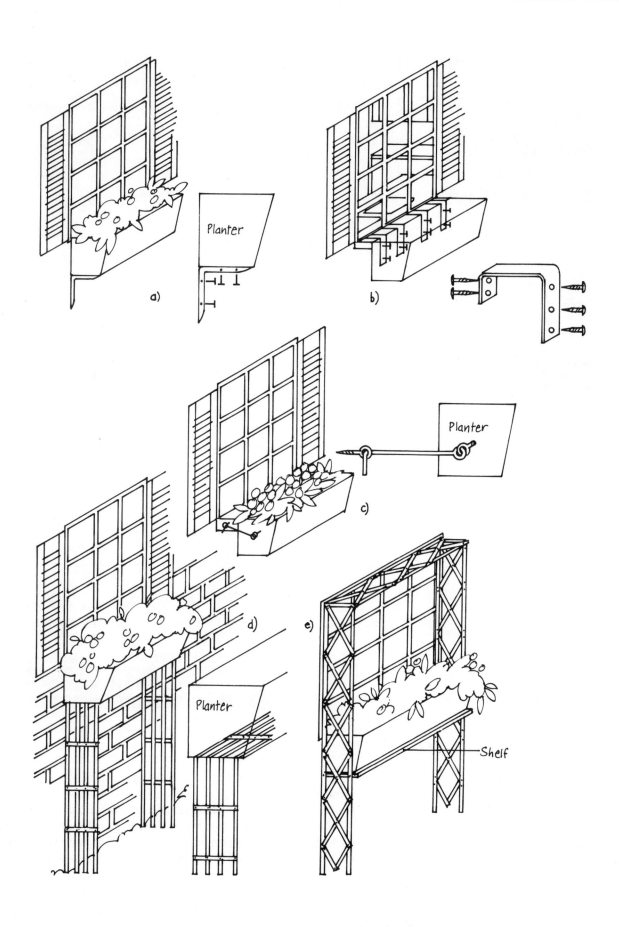

Planter

a)

Planter

b)

Planter

c)

d)

e)

Planter

Shelf

Wooden trough planter used with various hanging planters turns kitchen alcove into a greenhouse. (Photo by the makers of Armstrong resilient flooring)

Ways to Install Window Planters—(a) Using brackets: select brackets that will closely match, but not exceed, the width of your window box. Screw the long ends directly to the exterior of your house, and attach the shorter ends to the underside of your planter box. If your home is made of brick, be sure to use masonry nails for a secure fit. (b) This planter box is attached to the window sill on the exterior side by means of brackets that span the sill and are nailed or screwed directly to the inside back of the planter box. This assembly does not interfere with opening or closing the window. (c) A simple screw hook and eye is used to attach planter box to window sill. For large boxes, several hooks may be required. (d) Legs have been built to support this window planter. Such methods of support can be made from wood that is secured to the bottom of the planter for at least a quarter of its length from either side. If necessary, secure entire assembly to the exterior of the house by means of screws or hooks, to prevent it from falling over. (e) A trellis made from lathing strips built around this window serves as the support system for a window planter. Planter here sits on shelves made to its exact width.

If your house has siding and you do not want to put a hole through it, consider building a shelf out from the window supported by clamps which come over the sill and attach to the inside of the window.

If a few inches of sill extend past the outside of your window, you can also use this for partial support and further secure your planter by large eye hooks anchored into your window frame.

A more elaborate method, but an effective one, involves building a trellis and attaching the window box to the sides of it.

Although window planters generally hold less soil than a large tree planter requires, they can be a hazard if not attached securely. Never trust a window ledge to hold a box without further anchoring, especially on a second or third floor. Gusts of wind, rain and your own hand working on the plants can cause a planter to shift its weight or to fall.

Fiberglass window planters, available in many sizes and colors, serve as liners for finished boxes, or as easy-to-move display planters. (Molded Fiber Glass Tray Co.)

How to Build Your Own Window Planter

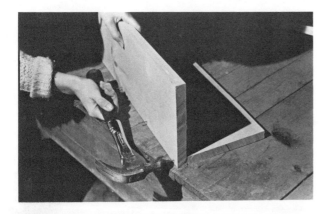

Making a Simple Window Planter—

Materials needed: 2 1 x 8 28 inch sides
1 1 x 8 28 inch base
2 1 x 8 8¾ inch ends
(In general, length of required materials should be determined by the width of your window.) Attach base to side, making sure ends

meet evenly. Nail other side to base, keeping pieces of box straight to meet evenly. Nail ends to bottom and sides. As with all joints, start nails on each side and pound them through in sequence after preliminary contact is made between two sides. Assemble box, drill drainage openings at intervals in the bottom. Allow at least two holes for every 4 inches of length. (Chris Maynard)

Window seat area beneath window becomes an ideal place for a planter. (Photo by the makers of Armstrong resilient flooring)

Drainage

Consider how your roof's drainage system will affect any outdoor window box. Many older houses do not have gutters to channel the water off to one side; in these homes, water simply runs off the roof and falls directly to the ground. Houses with gables and dormers may shed water from the roof by sending it down in torrents from the lowest common point on the roof. Either case may mean that your window planter will be subjected to floods that will batter your plants and wash out the soil.

If you do not have an effective gutter system, consider using an awning that is attached to the upper part of your window frame. Awnings of all kinds are sold at home decorating shops. Another solution is to install a length of gutter on the roof directly above your planter. It is not difficult to reroute water and defuse potential damage.

Before installing your planter, watch where the rain does drain off your roof, and determine the safest, most protected places for a window box.

USING WINDOW PLANTERS INDOORS

If you do not think you have a place to use a window planter outdoors, perhaps there is a place for one inside your home.

There are many different ways to incorporate planters into a window design. They can be used to highlight a sunny windowsill, to accentuate a window from the outside, and to take advantage of valuable, well-lit space. If you have a window that provides good light, plan a narrow box planter to create some new gardening space.

Before deciding on the style that bests fits your space, do a spot check of the hardware and mechanism for opening and closing your windows. Installed planters should never make it difficult to reach window clasps or pulls, or interfere with the sash. To avoid any problems, position a planter out from a window, or under it, rather than directly against it.

In older houses, windowsills frequently jut out as much as 8 to 10 inches from the window. This sort of built-in ledge forms an excellent shelf to support an indoor window box. Window seats can also be good places on which to rest a box filled with plants.

Installation

If no means to support a window box exists, here are several other installation methods you can try.

To build a windowsill or shelf under an existing window, cut a piece of wood the length of your win-

dow and the width of the planter you want to use. Attach it as you would a shelf, with either brackets or metal tracking. Or, build a small table—a base with legs that will offer support. Using screws, nails or glue, attach the table to the windowsill so it does not wobble or come away from the wall.

If the planter has a surface to which wood will adhere, build rectangular legs under your planter for support.

If your window frame is recessed to a depth of 6 inches or more, attach a window planter at the top of the window. Build a shelf across the window to hold the planter, or attach brackets or other supports to keep it in place. Fill the planter with trailing plants.

The molding at the top of the window provides the option of installing a hanging window box, supported much the same way a child's swing would be. Run two or more lengths of chain or cord from the top of your window frame to attach as support for the window box.

If you have windows that come all the way down to the floor, a planter box built to the width of the glass is an effective touch. As with all other window planters used in the home, make provision for drainage. An ideal way to do this is to use individually potted plants. Fill the bottom of the box with several inches of small stones. Place the separate pots in it and fill around them with additional stones. Your window planter will then look like a well-planned unit, rather than a jumbled collection of pots.

Be sure also that the window you choose receives at least four hours of good sunlight every day. Avoid areas that are shaded by trees (in the early spring, it is easy to underestimate the shade a tree will provide when its leaves are fully developed) or by other buildings.

Additional Locations

Here are some suggestions for other places to put planter boxes:

Kitchen Sink Area: If you have a window over your sink and at least five inches between the two, consider a built-in planter box that is level with the bottom of the window. Plants love the moisture from a sink area, and if you have a spray hose attachment, watering them becomes easy.

Alcove Area: An alcove or a small area defined by two walls that also has a window—an entranceway or hallway—offers a good window box location. Consider a planter box filled with trailing plants for a special effect.

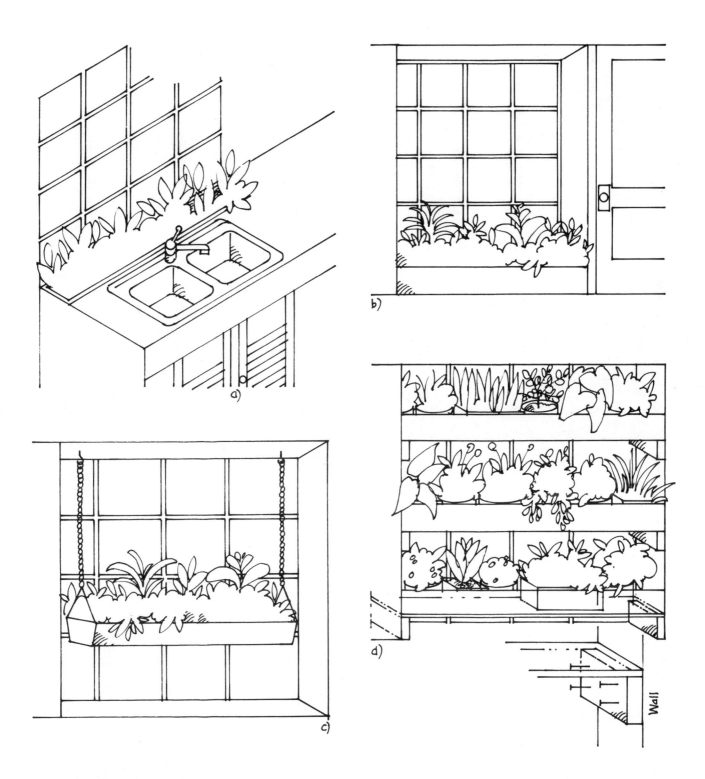

Ways to Use Window Planters in the House—*(a) Planter built in between window and kitchen sink provides attractive extra room for an herb garden or an assortment of small house plants. (b) In front of a floor-to-ceiling window. (c) Window planter mounted on hooks screwed into underside of window frame molding functions the same way as a child's swing. Hooks can suspend planter by chains or rope supports. Planters so installed can be easily re-moved for transplanting. This method works with any wooden window, since hooks are secured directly into wood that is sup-ported by the window frame itself. (d) Shelves built to span a window in several places are simply rested on small blocks of wood screwed into the window frame on the interior side. Both shelves and planters can be removed at any time.*

Metal shelves spanning dining area window create space for numerous house plants, without requiring any permanent installation of individual planters. (Photo by the makers of Armstrong interior furnishings)

Glass shelves secured with a minimum of hardware turn well-lit window into an exciting display area for growing plants. (Photo by the makers of Armstrong interior furnishings)

Stairway: A stairway with a window on the landing or at the top of the stairs can be an unusual but attractive site for a window box. Plants grown within traffic routes are rarely neglected, since they are so frequently seen.

Look around your house to determine what other window areas might be especially suitable for window boxes.

Other Types of Window Planters

In addition to the classic window boxes, several other kinds of planters are used in windows. Some of these include:

Hanging Window Garden: This planter features wrought-iron brackets and plastic or glass trays. The brackets simply clip on to the window to support

The humidi-tray, a window planter that holds several individual plants, contains a system to regulate their moisture. Trays come in various sizes to fit most standard window sills. (BEH Housewares Corp.)

Small window greenhouses can be installed in any size window.
(Lord & Burnham)

vertical supports. Available in green and white plastic, they can also be used as wall planters.

Gallery Window Shelf: Bordered by a decorative fence to prevent plants from dropping off the edges, this planter shelf comes in several lengths. Nailed to the window sill, it does not interfere with the window mechanism.

Shelf Units: Various kinds of shelves lend themselves to use as planter units. Consider glass shelving for maximum light dispersal, or ready-made units, available in plastic or wire.

Window Greenhouses: A newer development in window planters, small, mini-greenhouses extend out from an existing window. They provide a greenhouse environment and offer additional growing room. You can buy window greenhouses to fit various sizes and kinds of windows, in kits to assemble yourself.

two or more trays of individual potted plants, and the trays prevent water from dripping. The entire planter can be easily disassembled.

Window Pole Stand: A pole that adjusts to fit windows from 28 inches to 80 inches is secured with a clamp. The planter has 3 arms. One is 9 inches long; and two are 12 inches long; all support 6-inch saucers. Three additional saucers hang from the arms. This style comes in white, black or chrome.

French Window Shelves: For use outdoors as well as in, these plastic shelves attach directly to the window. They feature two horizontal shelves and four curved

5

Outdoor Planters for Special Effects

Some people shy away from the word "landscaping," fearing it to be a special talent known only to those who spend hours designing gardens and planning lots. But a personal kind of landscaping is possible with planters that you buy or build yourself.

WHY A PLANTER?

Before you invest any money in outdoor planters, be sure they are an answer to your needs. If you simply want to have some trees growing in your yard, the most

Gardening with planters creates flexibility as to where you can grow plants; note in how many places in this photograph planters bring growing space into areas that would otherwise be totally without soil. (California Redwood Association)

Three planters placed in a line break up space of large patio area and help guide traffic into more orderly patterns. (California Redwood Association)

practical step is to buy seedlings and plant them. The more plants you can place directly in the ground, the less care you will have to give them.

Watering and transplanting are two necessities that go hand in hand with planter gardening. But there are many other advantages to using planters.

Advantages

Mobility: If you live in a climate that has severe winters, a planter lets you keep a citrus tree or tropical shrub outside during the summer, but move it indoors or to another place during the winter. Planters with wheels provide the opportunity for moving plants in and out of the house as the seasons—or your moods—change. If your outdoor area includes chairs or a dining

arrangement, show off your flowering plants by moving them into view when they are blooming, and off to a place of lesser prominence when they are not in color.

Compensating for Poor Soil: If your backyard is a sandy beach, or a rocky desert area, planters enable you to grow plants that would otherwise not survive under local conditions. Adjust planter soil mixes to support plants not suitable to your native soil.

Serving As Functional Objects: Since planters occupy visible space above ground, they function as pieces of outdoor furniture or other service items—gates, walls or barriers. A row of planters directs or reroutes traffic whereas a line of spaced-out trees or a hedge might not.

Planters are Self-Contained: You can build a planter into areas where trees or shrubs could not be located.

Planters let you garden on stone patios, cement walkways and asphalt driveways.

WHERE TO USE PLANTERS

With the above considerations in mind, think about your own yard or patio space and ways to improve or change it by using planters.

Outside Uses

Solve Parking Problems: If you have a large driveway, planters may solve parking congestion. Install wooden boxes at eight or nine-foot intervals to act as directional barriers for cars.

Block Off Slopes: A drop-off or slope on your property, even one as slight as eight inches, can be a sudden surprise for anyone who is not prepared for it. A planter eliminates the potential danger posed by such an incline. Use a long, single planter or several smaller individual planters, placed either just before or just after the drop off. If your slope is accentuated by a patio, consider using planters to show where the patio ends and another ground level begins.

For Privacy: If a part of your yard is not as private as you would like it, planters can close it in or serve as substitute barriers until a planted hedge or row of trees has reached maturity. Use several of the same kind of planters in a row, or build long planter boxes and fill them with bushy plants.

To Create Borders: Along the edge of a driveway or walkway, planters help soften the abrupt meeting of concrete or asphalt with grass.

Guides for Traffic Flow: Create walkways and walls in some areas by using a row of planters, especially effective in a patio area where you want to avoid distraction from all sides. Let planters define spaces, and cut down on the choices that people have for entering an area. Several planters placed randomly in an open space

Baskets of hanging fuchsia plants turn an otherwise plain wall into an attention stopper. (Merry Gardens, Camden, Maine)

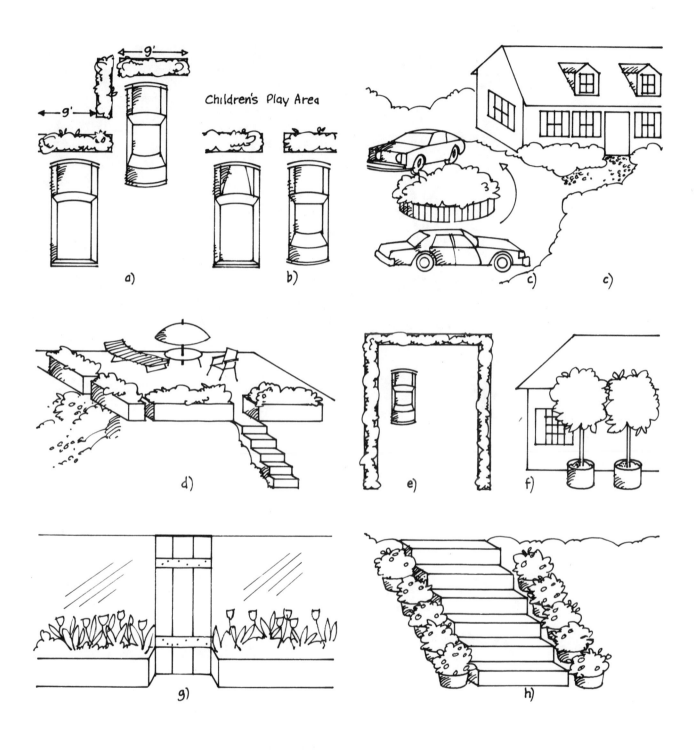

Using Planters Outdoors for Special Effects—*(a) Three planters spaced out in this driveway eliminate overparking by forming two separate parking bays. (b) This parking area depends on planters to cordon off a children's safe play area. (c) Houses with circular driveways are set off by round, centrally placed planters that keep traffic moving in just one direction. (d) Sloping sides around patio area are blocked off by a boundary of planters. (e) A continuous line of planters gracefully divides a driveway from a lawn. (f) Two planters save a bare wall from looking stark and neglected. (g) Planters on either side of a door frame picture windows and eliminate danger of a small child colliding with hard-to-see window glass. (h) Planters in two rows line stairway, and take away look of bare ground on either side.*

Views during two seasons show how planters can successfully be used to block off a slope, and to separate one area of the yard from another. (New York State College of Agriculture and Life Sciences at Cornell University)

Large planter adds drama, and helps camouflage wooden fence behind it. (California Redwood Association)

also decrease activity in a given space—an important consideration if you have children or pets. A circular driveway in front of a house can also be made more functional by a planter that keeps cars moving in the same direction.

As Camouflage: A planter with a climbing vine or trellis attached to it disguises a drainpipe or a crack in an above-ground foundation wall. Select a plant that readily climbs up whatever surface you have.

Hide a View: If there is a view to block, consider doing it with a planter. Large, leafy trees planted in sizable tubs obscure even the most unsightly scene—be it a nearby building or a vacant lot.

Make a Bare Wall Interesting: If your home or garage presents a blank wall, make it more interesting by adding a row of planters. Repeat the same combination of plant and planter for an effective design.

Break up Large Open Spaces: Large courtyards or patio areas that seem to pose landscaping problems by their size are neatly divided with planters.

Emphasize Windows: Floor-to-ceiling windows, especially those on either side of an entryway, pose a threat to active children, who may not realize that they are there. A planter box at the base of such a window, or a single planter in front of one, can safely separate it from passing traffic.

Beautify an Entryway: Front door or back, planters on either side of a door or in a row leading up a walkway, set off an entrance or form a path.

6

Planters for Aquatic Plants

Water gardening opens up another dimension in the use of planters. Start out with a simple tubful of water lilies, or expand your plans to include fish, statuary and waterfalls. How elaborately you try your hand with water plants is up to you, but some basic rules apply to any aquatic planter, no matter how large.

BASIC REQUIREMENTS

Whatever you grow—and there are many kinds of plants to try—be sure to maintain an ecological balance so the water remains clear, free from scum and algae. The larger your planter, the more problems that can arise from algae accumulation.

Solutions

To keep water gardens clean, Carol and Bill Uber of Van Ness Water Gardens in Upland, California, suggest that you maintain the necessary balance in planters by putting in these items:

Oxygenating Grasses: Ranging from stemmed and grass-like to ornamental varieties, these plants grow submerged. They give off oxygen and absorb carbon dioxide, present in planters in the form of decaying material. Since algae require carbon dioxide to grow, the grasses provide competition and thus check algae growth.

Water Lilies: Available in many sizes, colors and varieties, lilies cover the surface of the water with their pads, forming a layer that helps keep oxygen from leaving the water. They also keep the water temperature cool and thus cut down on the speed at which waste materials decay.

Snails: Water snails are scavengers that feed on decaying material and algae. They sweep clean any surfaces they use as feeding grounds.

Fish: Fish act as a control element because they can thrive in water gardens by feeding on mosquito larvae and insects.

Chemicals: If necessary, use a chemical control to keep algae growth at a minimum, especially in newly planted water gardens, before an ecological balance has a chance to get established. Select a controlling agent from a water gardening supply shop and carefully follow the directions.

The Ubers urge their customers to realize what a water garden really is: "It is important to remember that you are attempting to create a delicate balance of nature in an artificial environment." Always keep in mind that plant and animal life must have a compatible relationship.

In the Ubers' formula for a balanced water garden, each square yard of surface should contain:

- Two bunches of oxygenating grasses
- One water lily—medium to large size
- Twelve water snails
- Two fish, 4 to 5 inches long

CHOOSING A PLANTER

Once you understand the elemental ingredients for a water garden, next decide what kind of planter to use and how to incorporate it into your living area.

Place a large tub on a patio or balcony and convert it into a thriving water garden. Or, look at your planters

Water gardens are a strikingly different way to enhance your property with planters. (Chris Maynard)

simply as containers to be submerged in a larger pool and thus remain out of sight. They should always be functional, able to remain in contact with water for long periods without swelling, cracking or coming apart.

Materials

Plastic: A simple plastic tub from a housewares department makes a suitable aquatic planter. Select one that is wider than it is deep, to avoid tipping and to prevent using unnecessary amounts of soil. Plastic planters designed specifically for use with water are available at shops that specialize in aquatic gardens. They range in size from 12 by 3 inches to 19 by 9 inches.

Metal: Galvanized tubs are also sold at centers that specialize in water gardens—and can also be found in hardware stores. They can be submerged in water gardens or used above ground and spray-painted. A standard size is 20 by 10 inches. Some are available in various colors with enameled finishes.

Clay: Although made of a porous material, clay pots can be used in water gardens. Select shapes with broad bases for the most secure anchoring. Clay is best suited to submerged uses, rather than as an above-ground water garden container, since it sweats off water over a period of time.

Wood: Wooden boxes can also be submerged in water gardens, if free of seams that allow soil to erode. For best results, line them with sheets of metal, cut to fit. Do not submerge redwood planters as they will bleed.

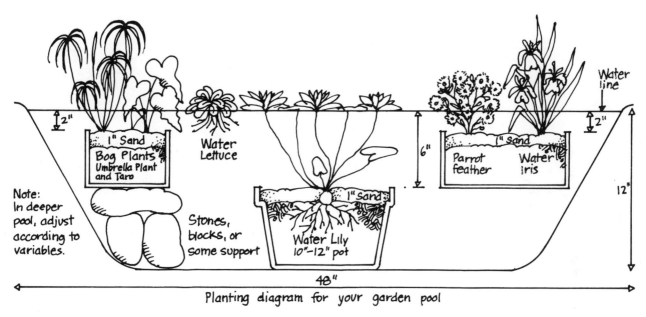

Planting diagram for your garden pool

A water garden constructed in a small pond or pool is actually nothing more than one large planter filled with several smaller ones. (Paradise Gardens, Whitman, Massachusetts)

USING PLANTERS IN POND OR POOL

A planter full of aquatic plants can be used above ground as an accent feature in small-scale landscaping. But for a more dramatic effect, and to experience truly the culture of aquatic plants, build a garden pool and submerge your planters in it.

Select a site away from trees to avoid the problem of leaves and other debris constantly falling into your pool. Most plants that grow in water require sun, so stay away from shady areas. Also consider the location of your septic tank or leaching field, if you have them, before you dig!

There are many ways to build a garden pool and it would be possible to devote an entire book to this aspect of gardening. We mention some basic kinds of pools here, to show you that they should be considered as simply large planters that you fill with smaller planters. Here are some types of pools that are widely available:

Plastic liners: An innovation in water gardening, polyvinyl chloride (PVC) liners are sheets of plastic that can be stretched into different shapes. Held in place by the weight of the water above them, they eliminate the need for forms, cement and reinforcing supports. (See installation diagram.)

Fiberglass pools: Available in standard sizes from 3 feet by 4 feet by 12 inches deep, holding 55 gallons, to 3 feet by 6 feet by 18 inches deep, holding 145 gallons, fiberglass pools come in many of the same shapes that swimming pools do. They are black, white, or aquamarine in color. Lightweight and easy to carry before filling, they are quickly installed and easily repaired.

Concrete: Although it is possible to build yourself a concrete pool, the technology that has led to prefabricated pools and liners makes this process the most time-consuming and also the most difficult for an amateur. Leaks caused by cracks formed during freezing winter months are a major problem with concrete pools built in northern climates. One advantage is that a concrete pool can be less costly to build.

BUILDING A CONCRETE GARDEN POOL

Before setting to work on a concrete pool which will, by its very nature, become a permanent part of your backyard landscaping, decide what varieties of aquatic plants you want to grow. This initial consideration will help you define the diameter and the depth your pool should be.

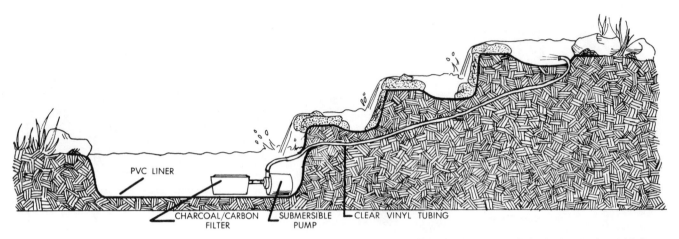

PVC LINER

CHARCOAL/CARBON   SUBMERSIBLE   CLEAR VINYL TUBING
FILTER   PUMP

PVC Liners—*PVC liners are pieces of plastic that can be molded to the contour of any sized hole in your garden. They facilitate creating a pond in very little time, with dependable results for years of enjoyment. (Van Ness Water Gardens, Upland, California)*

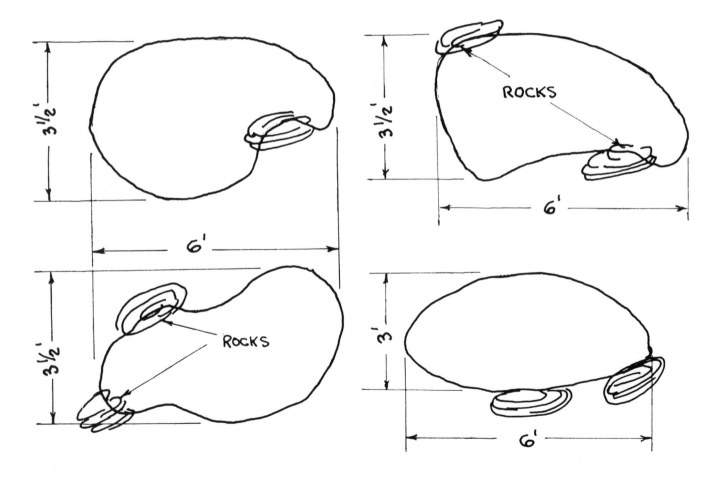

Garden pools can be built in free-form shapes and the edges lined with rocks or precast concrete slabs. Boulders can be added for accent.

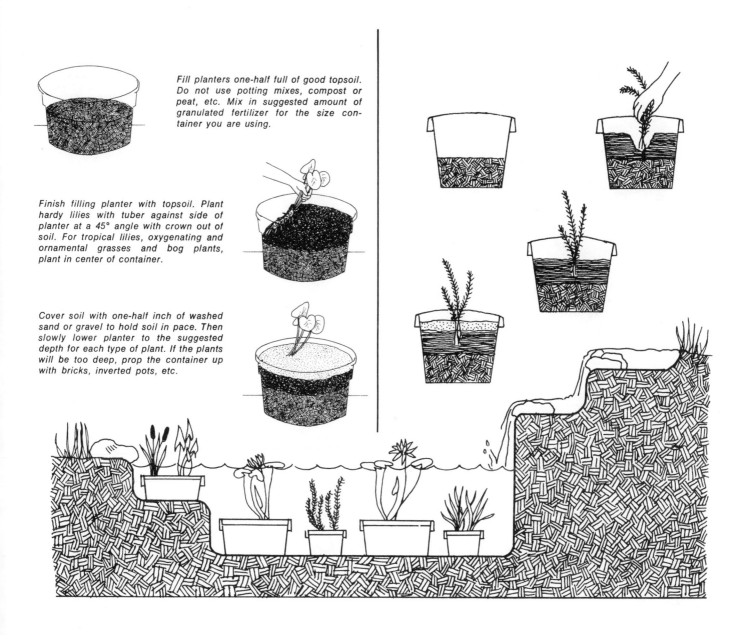

Fill planters one-half full of good topsoil. Do not use potting mixes, compost or peat, etc. Mix in suggested amount of granulated fertilizer for the size container you are using.

Finish filling planter with topsoil. Plant hardy lilies with tuber against side of planter at a 45° angle with crown out of soil. For tropical lilies, oxygenating and ornamental grasses and bog plants, plant in center of container.

Cover soil with one-half inch of washed sand or gravel to hold soil in pace. Then slowly lower planter to the suggested depth for each type of plant. If the plants will be too deep, prop the container up with bricks, inverted pots, etc.

How to Plant Water Gardens *(Van Ness Water Gardens, Upland, California)*

Small water lilies thrive in a pool that is as narrow as 3 feet across, but healthy plants will require a depth of approximately 2 feet.

Pockets or ledges can be installed to allow for plants that could not adapt to this depth.

To dig a simple bowl-shaped pool, excavate 3 feet in the center, and slope the sides gradually for a tapered depth as you leave the center. The more gradual the change in height in your pool, the less likely you will be to require forms. A rise of 1 foot within the distance of 2 feet will set without support.

First lay the drain pipe, blocked with newspaper or rags to prevent clogging. Next, lay concrete to a thickness of 6 inches, starting at the bottom and working your way up the sides. Halfway into the middle of the pour, stop to lay a layer of reinforcement. This can be

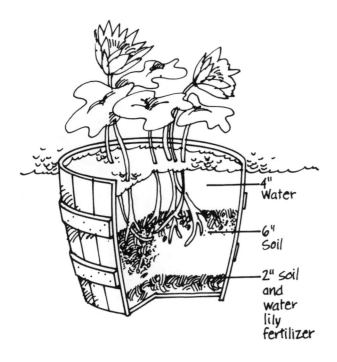

Cross-section of water planter shows suggested depths of soil, water and fertilizer for water lily. (Paradise Gardens, Whitman, Massachusetts)

6 x 6 to 10 x 10 welded wire fabric or 3/8 inch reinforcing bars. For a cobblestone surface, place a layer of stones into the concrete before it has set.

As soon as the concrete has set, fill the pool with water to cure the surface.

Since the first water in the pool will absorb alkali from the concrete, plan to empty and refill the pool several times in the first month to allow complete absorption of the alkali into the water. Then plant your selections.

HOW TO PLANT A WATER GARDEN

If your planter is to be submerged in a pool or pond, it requires some attention at planting time.

In place of standard soil mixes, use only topsoil without peat moss, vermiculite or other mixed ingredients. This prevents particles lighter than the water from accumulating on the surface.

Fill the planter half full of soil. Add fertilizer according to package directions (use only fertilizer that has been designed for use with water plants). Cover the roots of your plant with soil and finish off the top layer

Requirements for Aquatic Plants

	Suggested Planter Size: width/depth	Suggested Soil Line Depth: below water
Water Lilies	15" X 5½" to 20" X 10"	6–8"
Oxygenating grasses	12" X 3" to 15" X 5½"	8" or more
Bog plants	7" X 15" to 20" X 10"	3–6"
Ornamental grasses	12" X 3" to 7" X 5"	4–8"
Lotus	20" X 10" to 15" X 5½"	6–8"
Small flowering plants	15" X 5½" to 12" X 3"	4–8"

of soil with about an inch of sand or gravel. Then lower the planter into the water.

To achieve varying heights in a pond or pool, place individual planters on blocks, on bricks, or even on legs that you have made extra sturdy. Individual planters give you the flexibility necessary to adjust different plants to different water depths.

The above suggestions have been taken from *Water Visions,* the booklet and catalogue from Van Ness Water Gardens (see Appendix).

AQUARIUMS AS PLANTERS

It is also possible to enjoy aquatic plants indoors by growing them in a simple aquarium—with or without the fish!

Standard fish tanks sold at pet shops and aquarium supply centers come in many sizes, from small, 5-gallon models to large ones that can hold 220 gallons. This latter size, 72 inches long, 24 inches wide and 30 inches high, can make a breathtaking planter when filled with healthy plants!

Be sure to achieve the same ecological balance indoors as that described earlier in this chapter for outdoor water gardens. Look into the various kinds of grasses, lilies and plants that are available. Also consult aquarium dealers for information on filter systems and water circulating mechanisms. Water that moves through a filter can be kept cleaner, and your plants will appear to wave and sway in the current.

7
Making Your Own Planters

The construction of larger, stationary planters, enables you to save money and enjoy a creative adventure at the same time.

The following pages present some plans for you to follow with guaranteed success; or, you may choose to go on from here and develop your own design. Whichever route you take, remember to keep the basic requirements of your planter in mind (see Chapter 1).

USING WOODS

Wood is the most common material from which to build your own planters. Check local newspapers for ads from nearby lumber yards, or compare prices among several places to find the best deals on available lumber. Most yards allow customers to inspect lumber before ordering. If you are planning on natural wood finishes, check the wood's color. Also avoid lumber that has many knots, that is warped, or that has obvious cracks and splits.

In general, woods fall into two categories: hardwoods and softwoods. Softwoods include mainly woods from conifers—pine, fir, cedar and redwood. Cheaper than hardwoods, they can be readily cut through, sanded and stained by even the novice builder. Most lumberyards have extensive quantities and sizes of various softwoods.

Hardwoods, including oak, maple and birch, are more expensive and more difficult to find in smaller lumber yards. Their frequently more aesthetically pleasing natural grains look well in planters in which the natural wood finishes are intended to show through. Novices should be extremely careful in work-

ing with hardwoods, since a wrongly placed nail or screw sometimes causes the board to crack.

Characteristics

Following are some characteristics of individual woods that are recommended for planter construction:

Redwood: Heart redwood, a premium cut from the tree, has the highest tolerance to moisture and thus makes the most durable planters. Other grades are suitable as well, but by using them you sacrifice longevity. Redwood resists decay and weathers gracefully. No exterior finish is required, but polyurethane brings out the highlights of the wood.

Cedar: As is true of redwood, cedar resists rotting on contact with moisture and can stand to go unfinished in even the dampest climates. To be safe, provide some further protection. Cedar gives off a lovely fragrance and is a delight to work with.

Pine: Readily available and suited to the most modest budget, pine is sold in several grades any of which can be fashioned into acceptable planters. For the smoothest finish, select number one or two grade pine. The wood can easily be cut with a hand saw, but must be carefully treated to resist decay.

Plywood: Economical to use, and sold in various grades, plywood offers the advantage of being a very strong wood; it is made from layers of thin sheets of wood bonded together for strength. However, the layers warp and separate on prolonged contact with even minimal moisture, so care should be taken to seal all edges with preservatives.

Other Materials: In addition to wood, you can choose from other materials for homemade planters. Fiber glass, plexiglass, plastic, brick, concrete, and stone all

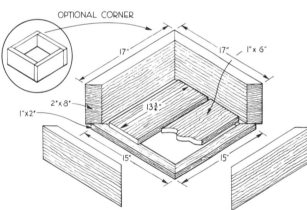

Patio Planter Box– *Redwood planter is designed to hold four 6-inch pots which could be changed at intervals. The two grades California Redwood Association recommends for planters are Clear All Heart for an even, architectural, luxurious appearance, and Construction Heart for a rustic, natural, economical product. (California Redwood Association)*

Large Redwood Planter Box–*Construction Heart redwood "packing crate" planter is easily assembled and adds a natural, rustic aspect to its environment. Redwood planters need no finish, but a water repellent could be applied to discourage extractive staining. Allow two weeks before planting to let toxic agents from water repellents become harmless. (California Redwood Association)*

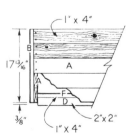

lend themselves to planter design, requiring varying initial outlays of money, energy and knowledge.

Suggestions to Keep in Mind

Wood is an easy material to work with. Widely available, versatile, an excellent insulator against the heat of the sun in all climates, wood lends itself to painting, staining and being covered with various fabrics and materials. Even a beginning carpenter can construct a satisfactory, though simple, planter from lengths of wood cut with a design in mind.

Wood requires some important preparatory considerations:

1. Waterproof any portion of the wood that will come in contact with either the soil or the weather. Choose from creosote, primer, copper naphthenate, tree sealant or asphalt paint. For the best results, treat surfaces before assembling the planter.

2. Use screws or nails that will not rust; stainless steel, aluminum or galvanized are best. Screws hold joints together more securely than nails, and they facilitate disassembling the planter should you decide to move it or to check the root system of your plant.

BUILDING YOUR OWN PLANTERS FROM SCRATCH

Patio Planter Box

A simple planter box, this one is designed to hold four individual 6 inch pots. It is ideal for herb gardens or for separate house plants that you may want to move outdoors in summer. If you choose, you can make a permanent display by removing the pots and planting directly in the box.

Materials needed

6 feet of 2 x 8 inch lumber for the sides
6 feet of 1 x 2 inch lumber for the bottom rim
28 inches of 1 x 6 inch lumber for the bottom

1. Cut side pieces as shown in diagram. Use mitre box to cut 450 degree angles, or make simple butt joints with straight, 90-degree cuts.

2. Nail or screw sides together. For best results, drive nails or install screws in pre-drilled holes.

3. Cut pieces for bottom rim and attach to the edges of the sides. Place them so each piece of the rim extends 3/4 inch beyond the inner side edges. What you are doing is making a shallow ledge for the bottom boards to rest upon.

4. Cut 1 x 6 boards to fit snugly across the bottom. Place them evenly inside the box, leaving spaces for drainage between them. Nail boards in place, or leave them unattached.

Large Redwood Planter Box

This planter is ideal for large trees and shrubs.

Materials needed

70 feet of 1 x 4 inch redwood for sides
6 feet of 2 x 2 inch redwood for bottom

1. Cut 1 x 4's into 20 boards, 22 1/2 inches long.

2. Put together five sets of sides and ends as illustrated.

3. Stack the five sets and measure the total height. Cut 1 x 4 verticals for the end frame and nail from the inside, using nails or screws at the ends of each of the five boards.

4. Cut horizontal end frame boards to fit and nail from the interior, alternating as shown in diagram.

5. Measure interior dimensions of the box. Cut two 2 x 2's approximately 21 inches long and two more approximately 19 1/4 inches long. Nail the 2 x 2 base with one nail at each corner.

6. Cut 1 x 4's 21 inches long. Space the boards approximately 1/8 inch apart and nail them to the base using two nails at each end of each board. The spaces will provide the planter's drainage.

7. Insert the base and bottom boards, leaving 3/8 inch of the base extended below the bottom. This will keep the bottom of the planter from resting on the ground.

8. Nail the 2 x 2 base into the bottom from the interior, using five nails per side.

Planter Bench

Materials needed

1 sheet 3/8 inch plywood
1 sheet 3/4 inch plywood
20 feet 2 x 2 wood
71 feet 2 x 4 inch wood

Planter boxes, garden seats and benches are easily built (plans available from Z-Brick). A wide variety of designs can be constructed using common lumber and Z-Brick, a lightweight decorative brick. Unlike those built with real masonry, the Z-Brick planters and benches can be easily moved around for storage.

This interesting, practical unit is about as easy to build as any planter can be. All it takes is a frame for a simple box, plus, one or two members to hold potted plants in either a plastic or a metal planter box. Cover with plywood or brick facing and you have a nice feature for garden or patio.

Planter Tubs

A small, lightweight and attractive planter for flowers or potted plants, this one can have a round or a square opening at the top. To make this into a real planter to hold the soil directly (rather than to hold a container that holds the soil) build an inner box and coat sides

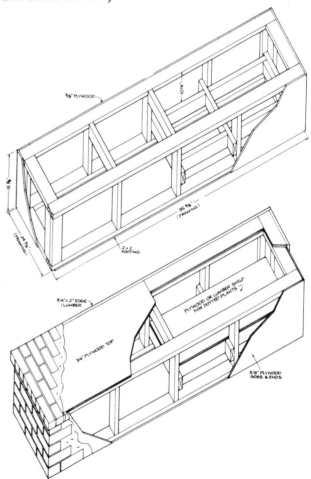

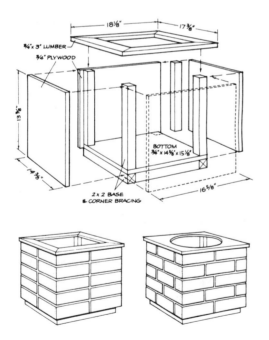

Planter benches are about as easy to build as anything can be. Vary the size if you wish but be careful to figure out even courses of Z-Brick to save unnecessary trimming. (Allow for 2-3/8 inch width plus about 5/8 inch of mortar per course). After building the frame, sheath with plywood having exterior type glue. Then just face with durable, weatherproof Z-Brick and seal. (Reproduced from plans offered by the Z-Brick Company, Woodinville, Washington)

Here's a small, lightweight and attractive planter tub for some of your favorite potted plants and flowers. Build the top with square opening or round and vary the size to fit your large pots. If you want to make this a real planter to hold soil and all, build an inner box of exterior type plywood and coat liberally with Z-Ment Adhesive Mortar. Add a drain hole or two and that should do the trick. Let Z-Ment dry for a week before filling with soil. (Reproduced from plans offered by the Z-Brick Company, Woodinville, Washington)

with mortar or a similar material. Drill several holes in the bottom to provide drainage.

Materials needed

1/2 sheet 3/4 inch plywood
10 feet 1 x 4 inch wood
10 feet 2 x 2 inch wood
1 1/2 cartons brick facings
1 gallon adhesive mortar
1 quart sealer

Planter Divider

This unusual planter design makes a container large enough to hold an array of potted plants and flowers that can then be arranged at will. It can furnish a private area in a large yard or enhance a patio or entryway.

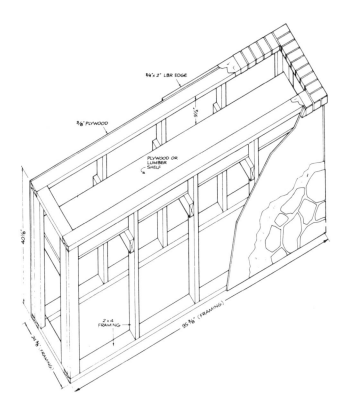

Somewhere in your home or garden, there is just the right spot for the handsome, practical planter/divider. The cutaway shows how frame is sheathed and finished. Sheathing should be plywood made with exterior type glue. Use construction adhesives as well as nails for maximum strength. The sturdy frame will then have great rigidity and will give you years of service indoors or out. (Reproduced from plans offered by the Z-Brick Company, Woodinville, Washington)

Materials needed

3 sheets of 3/8 inch plywood
1 piece plywood 16 3/8 x 92 3/8 inches
74 feet 2 x 4 inch wood
21 feet 3/4 x 2 inch wood

Mediterranean-Style Planter

This octagonal wishing well is based on an elaborate but striking design. The height can be varied at will by adjusting the length of the supporting members.

Materials needed

2 sheets of 1/2 inch plywood
1 piece 18 x 32 inches of 3/4 inch plywood
60 feet 2 x 2 inch wood
26 feet 2 x 4 inch wood
2 ornamental iron columns
4 conduit clips
shakes for roof

Square Wishing Well

The square version of the wishing well is a simpler one to build and is based upon a straightforward design. This model requires no special tools, and all materials are readily available at even the smallest lumber yard.

Materials needed

2 sheets 1/2 inch plywood
1 piece 33 x 30 inch 3/4 inch plywood for shelf
65 feet 2 x 4 inch wood
14 feet 2 x 10 inch wood
1 piece 1 x 4 inch wood
1 piece 4 x 4 inch wood
1 piece 2 inch dowel shakes or shingles for roof

Screen Planter

A very useful planter, this one combines a screen for privacy and shading with a double-sided planter that can be used for all kinds of growing plants.

Materials needed

2 sheets 3/8 inch plywood
1 sheet 3/4 inch plywood
18 feet 1 x 4 inch wood
50 feet 2 x 2 inch wood
28 feet 2 x 4 inch wood
6 1/4 x 4 inch bolts

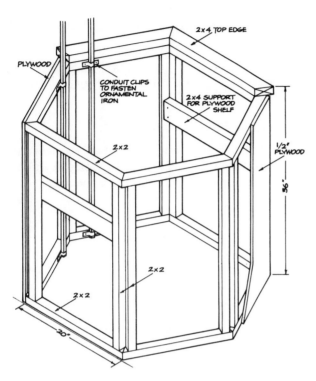

Here are the plans for the basic Mediterranean style planter. If you have some ability with tools you may wish to change the dimensions to build a larger unit. The plans can be modified readily. (Reproduced from plans offered by the Z-Brick Company, Woodinville, Washington)

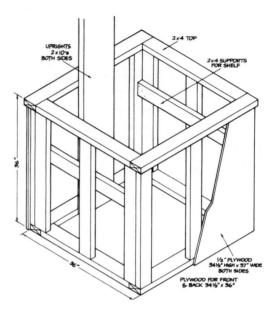

This attractive, decorative well is of simple, straightforward design. All the materials are from your lumber dealer and can be put together with ordinary hand tools. (Reproduced from plans offered by the Z-Brick Company, Woodinville, Washington)

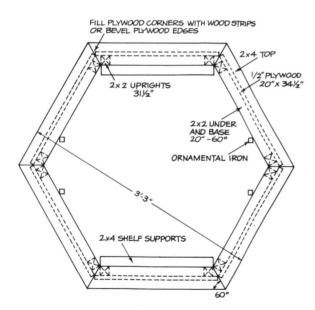

These drawings give measurements and positions for the framing assembly. Cover with plywood made with exterior type glue. For great strength and rigidity, fasten materials with Construction Adhesive as well as with nails. (Reproduced from plans offered by the Z-Brick Company, Woodinville, Washington)

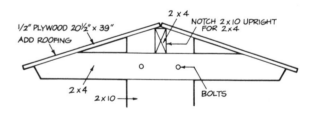

ROOF DETAIL FOR BOTH PLANTERS. This basic roof structure can be used on either the square or the octagonal planter. Height can be varied to taste by adjusting length of supporting members. Usually, 6 inch or 6-1/2 inch to eaves seems about right. To fasten, just bolt 2 x 4 joists to 2 x 10 uprights or to ornamental iron supports as case may be. Roof should be finished with shakes and a simple wood or sheet metal weather cap added along ridge. (Reproduced from plans offered by the Z-Brick Company, Woodinville, Washington)

OTHER PLANTERS YOU CAN BUILD

In addition to planters that you build yourself, there are hundreds of objects that can be made into satisfactory planters with just a little time and imagination. Trunks, boxes, barrels, sinks, ice boxes, cabinets, coolers, TV sets, radio cabinets, sewing machine tables, and even

Here's an ingenious combination—a screen/planter. This planter on both sides of the screen functions as a counterbalance to offset wind. And the screen is an attractive backdrop for the flowers in the planter. It also can serve as protection against wind or to add privacy to a secluded spot in the garden. (Reproduced from plans offered by the Z-Brick Company, Woodinville, Washington)

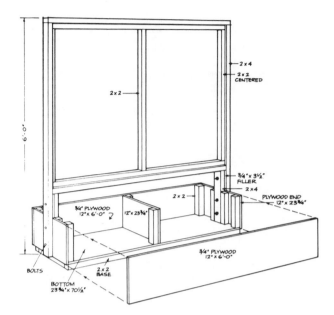

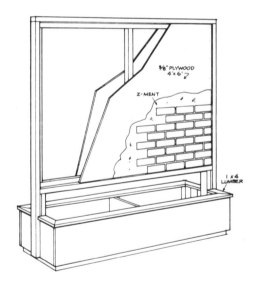

wheelbarrows and row boats all have the potential to become attractive and useful planters.

Following are a few suggestions for planters you can make yourself from other items. Look around your house, in your basement, garage and attic and surely you'll think of at least one more!

Wire Planters

Especially suited for use outdoors since they cannot avoid a certain amount of dripping after watering, wire planters can be made from wire baskets sold at garden centers or from recycled items—bicycle baskets, fruit and vegetable baskets or even chicken wire supports left over from elaborate centerpieces.

1. Soak a quantity of peat moss in water until it is well saturated; it should be at the point where it can be wrung out like a sponge.

2. Pull off chunks that are just larger than the wire mesh openings on the planter shape you are using. Squeeze the chunks out and gently begin at the top to force them into place. (They should act much like a damp sponge and spring into place when your fingers release them.)

3. Work your way around the wire shape until every space is lined with moss. Then add another layer on the

inside—enough to hold soil in and seal any cracks that may remain.

4. Your basket is now ready for planting. Starting at the bottom, poke holes through the moss and insert seedlings or cuttings. Work your way around, allowing several inches between plants, and continue to the top.

5. Fill the basket with soil, being careful to leave the seedlings' roots intact. Water and hang in a shady place for a day or two until root growth has begun, then move to a sunny place.

Redwood heartwood planter will resist rot and decay, can be used without liner or preservative. Redwood will take and hold any finish beautifully, can be left to weather naturally to a tannish gray or a coat of water repellent may be applied every one or two years to maintain the natural color and minimize the effects of moisture. (California Redwood Association)

Clear All Heart redwood indoor/outdoor planter's angled sidewalls give it a large capacity. (California Redwood Association)

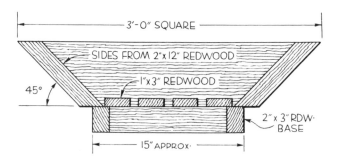

Abruptly angled sidewalls make this planter large enough for a small tree. Care should be taken when the mitered corners are cut. (California Redwood Association)

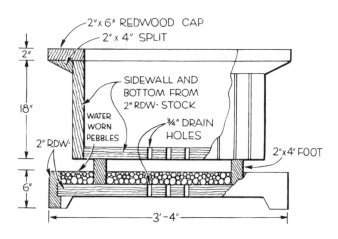

Tongue and groove 2 inch x 6 inch Clear All Heart redwood with 1/4 inch channels, routed with a Dado head 3 inches apart, was used to side this planter. (California Redwood Association)

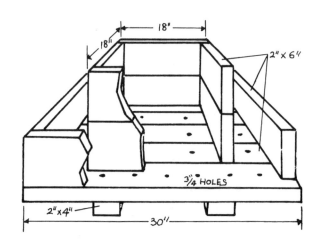

TIERED PLANTER BOX

Quantity	Size	Length
7	2 x 6	6 in.
1	2 x 4	6 in.

No. 12 Galvanized Nails
(Louisiana Pacific Corporation)

PLANTER BOX GROUP

TRIANGLE PLANTER BOX *(Make four)*

Quantity	Size	Length	
2	2 x 6	17 in.	Sides
1	2 x 6	24 in.	Sides
1	2 x 6	17 in.	Cut corners
2	2 x 8	12 in.	For bottom
1	2 x 4	24 in.	Cleats for
1	2 x 4	11 in.	Bottom

SQUARE PLANTER BOX

2	2 x 4	17 in.	Cleats
3	2 x 6	17 in.	Bottom
2	2 x 6	17 in.	
2	2 x 6	14 in.	Sides

(Louisiana Pacific Corporation)

FOOTED PLANTER

Quantity	Size	Length	
4	2 x 6	36 in.	For top
8	2 x 6	24 in.	For sides
4	2 x 6	21 in.	For bottom stand
2	2 x 4	30 in.	Stand bottom
4	2 x 4	15 in.	Stand sides

Coated 10 penny nails
(Louisiana Pacific Corporation)

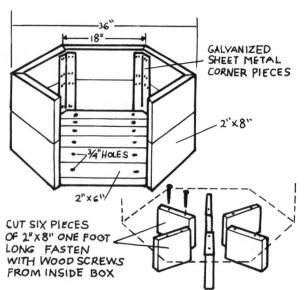

GALVANIZED
SHEET METAL
CORNER PIECES

2"x8"

¾"HOLES

2"x6"

CUT SIX PIECES
OF 2"x8" ONE FOOT
LONG FASTEN
WITH WOOD SCREWS
FROM INSIDE BOX

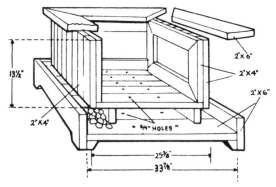

ELEVATED PLANTER BOX

Quantity	Size	Length	
2	2 x 8	10 ft.	Sides
1	2 x 8	6 ft.	Feet
3	2 x 8	6 ft.	Bottom
6	Galvanized metal corner pieces		

No. 6 box galvanized nails
3 in. wood screw or No. 10 nails
(Louisiana Pacific Corporation)

GRAVEL TRAY PLANTER BOX

Quantity	Size	Length	
2	2 x 4	22-3/8 in.	Cleats
4	2 x 6	22-3/8 in.	Bottom
4	2 x 4	22-3/8 in.	Inside
4	2 x 4	12 in.	End frame
4	2 x 4	19-3/8 in.	Side frames
28	2 x 4	13-1/2 in.	Sides
4	2 x 6	36 in.	Top rail
6	2 x 6	33-7/8 in.	Bottom lower box
4	2 x 6	38 in.	Side rails lower box
1	2 x 6	18 in.	Cleats lower box

NOTE: Split 18 in. 2 x 4 into 2 cleats at 45° angle.
box 36 x 36 outside
(Louisiana Pacific Corporation)

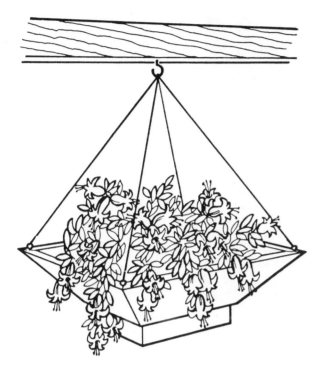

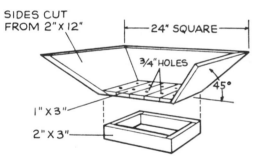

SIDES CUT
FROM 2"x 12"

24" SQUARE

3/4" HOLES

45°

1" X 3"

2" X 3"

HANGING PLANTER BOX

A cleverly recycled piece of driftwood forms attractive and unusual planter for a strawberry begonia plant. (Chris Maynard)

An old barrel turned into a planter holds a stunning succulent, called a donkey-tail sedum for its unusual strings of leaves. (Chris Maynard)

A hanging basket lined with sphagnum moss can be used for many different kinds of plants. (Chris Maynard)

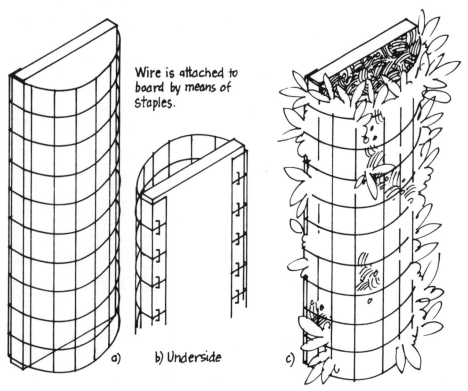

Wire is attached to board by means of staples.

a) b) Underside c)

A wire cylinder allows you to grow several feet worth of plants in a patio corner, or in other limited space. (a) To a board that is 3 or 4 feet long, attach a piece of wire the same length and no more than 18 inches wide. (b) Cross-section view shows staples used to secure wire to board. (c) Fill in spaces with moist sphagnum moss, and plant seedlings of your choice in each space.

Wire Cylinders

Vertical planters are an excellent way to utilize limited growing space.

1. Select a board that is cut to the height you desire for your planter; it should be no wider than 6 inches and no narrower than 3 inches. A workable height is 3 or

4 feet. Cut a piece of plastic the same size as the board, which will be used to hold the soil in place.

2. Also obtain a piece of wire cut to the same length as the board, and to a width no greater than 18 inches, no less than 10 inches.

3. Fold the wire into a semi-circle and staple each end to the under side of the board. Fill the cylinder with moss, as described earlier in this section or line it with a piece of black plastic. Poke holes through the plastic or through the moss and plant your seedlings in the spaces. Fill the cylinder with soil and water carefully, making sure nothing is washed out.

Silverware Tray Planter

A divided plastic tray, formerly used to keep silverware organized, can serve as an interesting planter for rooting cuttings, small plants, herbs or succulents.

Make several small drainage holes in the bottom. Fill tray with soil, vermiculite or sand. Attach a wooden base to the under side to keep the soil from filtering through. Plant the items of your choice in rows, and water.

Tire Planter

As unlikely as it may sound, an old automobile tire can be transformed into an attractive and functional planter.

1. Place the tire on its side so it is stable. Draw a design on the side facing you, using latex paint or a soft wax crayon. (The design can be semicircles, points or a combination of the two, but keep it relatively simple and such that each part of the design can be cut out in one piece.)

2. With a sharp knife or heavy, singled-edged blade, cut out your design markings.

Indoors, a leafy tree has been planted in another old barrel. Note ring mark on floor to left of planter; to avoid these, keep a saucer under such a planter at all times. (New York State College of Agriculture and Life Sciences at Cornell University)

3. Upend the tire and turn it inside out. The planter is ready to be filled with soil and planted. If you wish to move it, attach a base to the bottom by wiring a piece of wood cut to size with several holes drilled in it. Note: an uncut tire can also be used as a planter. Simply paint it and fill it with soil.

Wagon Wheel-Ladder

Wooden wagon wheels can be attractive planters, especially for herb gardens that require organization to prevent their growing wild. Ladders with wooden rungs also work well for this design.

1. Paint or stain the wheel or ladder to have the finish you desire, to prevent decay on contact with the ground.

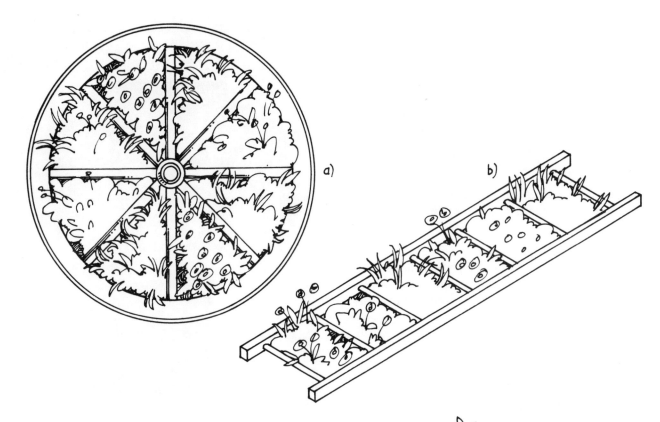

Wagon Wheel and Ladder Planter—*(a) To recycle an old wagon wheel, first paint it with enamel or a moisture-resistant substance. Then clear a space in your yard and place wheel on bed of finely sifted soil. Plant herbs or low flowering plants, a different kind within each space, for an exciting and unusual garden. (b) Following the same idea as that for the wagon wheel, select different herbs or flowering plants to adorn the spaces between rungs of an old ladder you have laid flat on the lawn.*

Strawberry Barrel

In a large barrel, approximately 50 gallons, drill holes in alternating layers, every 8 inches, in rows 4 inches apart. Fill the barrel with soil, and insert individual strawberry plants into each opening.

Presto Planter, an attractive California redwood plant stand, is a family do-it-yourself project. Carton-packaged with easy instructions, its 22 precision-notched parts press together for rigid construction, without nails or glue. Features include four-level adjustable plant platform, opening to accommodate a 9-inch pot, choice of 18, 24 or 30-inch heights and suitability for indoor or outdoor use. See manufacturer's list for address. (Eagle Forest Products)

An unusual planter kit, this one from a line of Makit and Bakit crafts, is constructed of stained glass. It comes in pieces that you put together and decorate yourself. (Quincrafts Corporation)

2. Select an area in your yard that receives good sun and cultivate it carefully, removing any weeds or rocks. Work on an area that is approximately the same size as the total area of the wheel or ladder.

3. Place the wheel or ladder over the area and work it into the soil until it is partially buried, but so that all the sections are still visible.

4. Plant herbs or flowers in the sections between spokes, and water.

Strawberry Barrel

Strawberries (and vegetables such as spinach and lettuce) grow readily in vertical columns of soil. A barrel with wooden sides, or the ready-made strawberry urn that is available in clay, function as excellent planters.

1. Select a large barrel—50 gallons or just a little smaller. Check local papers for sales on used whiskey barrels or old cider kegs. Stay away from metal barrels,

as they become very hot when struck by direct sunlight.

2. With a keyhole saw, drill holes in alternating layers around the circumference, every 8 inches, and in rows at least 4 inches apart. Also drill several holes in the base of the barrel for drainage.

3. Fill the barrel with soil, tamping it down slightly as you go, so the first rain won't wash it all away.

4. Insert individual strawberry plants into each opening, pushing the roots gently into the soil and making sure they are covered with earth.

5. Water the soil from the top.

Planter Kits

Do-it-yourself planter kits open up another area of planters that can be made easily in the home, as a family project if you so choose. They consist of pieces of wood cut to fit, and come with easy-to-follow directions. Some models contain from 22 to 40 pieces, all precision-notched so you can connect them without nails or glue. (See photos for some examples of these planters. Consult the Manufacturers List for others.)

8

New Designs in Planters

Clay and plastic pots, redwood tubs, and aluminum window boxes are used widely in this country today. They form the backbone of container gardening, and every serious gardener has turned to one at some time or another simply to fulfill a basic horticultural function.

But the new designs and creative thoughts that are so much a part of American technology have not failed to touch the manufacturing of planters and the materials from which they are made. Many companies have taken basic shapes—squares, cylinders and rectangles—and incorporated these into exciting new forms that can be used alone or in groupings.

New styles of planters highlight the role of a container in both indoor and outdoor areas. But in most cases, while they show off new materials, new colors and new designs, they also enhance, rather than overwhelm, the plants that are used in them.

The following pages feature some new concepts in planter design, suitable for use in your home.

Self-watering Planters: Since watering is a critical factor in caring for plants, a great innovation in planter manufacturing is a line of containers that are self-watering. They include a large water reservoir, with a wick that supplies water to the soil as demanded by the plants themselves. These planters have a vertical filling column which allows free flow of water, and many come equipped with a gauge so you can tell how much water has been added. Self-watering planters are available in many different styles, colors and materials.

Duraclay Planters: A material widely used by Group Artec, Duraclay is a fusion of clay and reinforced plastic. It is unbreakable, resists damage from freezing temperatures, and is available through decorators and designers in many shapes and forms. Some of the newest shapes are geometric designs that cannot be as

readily produced in high-fired ceramics. Duraclay planters used indoors do not require drainage openings, but they should be lined with gravel to keep plant roots from sitting in accumulated water. Outdoor planters should have a drainage opening.

Polypropylene Planters: Accepted by the London Design Centre, these plastic planters are tough, yet pliable—so strong that they can support your weight, so flexible that they can be pressed together until their edges touch. Lighter than clay and virtually unbreakable, they require less water than many other kinds of planters and are available as pots, as hanging planters, or as patio planters, up to 15 inches wide and ten-and-a-half inches high. They come in dark green and black.

Featherock Planters: Featherock is made from hardened volcanic ash (pumice) and offers many advantages as a planter material. Although there is nothing new about pumice itself, its application to planters is a recent concept. A plant that has been set into a Featherock planter cannot be overwatered, since the material is porous; this means no soggy roots, no waterlogged plants. Featherock comes in 2-inch-thick slabs or in unshaped chunks. You simply bring it home, moisten it, take a hammer and chisel, and set to work carving out a space to hold whatever plant you have in mind. To find sources of Featherock in your area, look in the yellow pages under "stone" or "masonry supplies."

Redwood Planters: As a material, redwood has been used for years in the planter industry, but some current designs reflect different methods of construction. In the most modern all-heart redwood planters, no nails or glue are used in the assembly. The individual parts of the planter are tongue-and-grooved, and steel hoops with iron lugs are used as reinforcement and support. Exterior surfaces are sanded and finished with sealer to give further protection against the weather.

Metal-finished Planters: Many new planter designs

Ranging from very small models for table top use to large units suited for grouping, these planters show some of the contemporary designs currently on the market. (Group Artec)

This self-watering planter features a water reservoir and regulatable water-feeder system to help reduce maintenance. Measuring 19 inches in diameter and 18 inches in height, this planter can hold a three-to-six month supply of water. (Architectural Supplements, Inc.)

include a shiny metal finish that provides special effects and can act as a mirror to reflect highlights in a room. Most finishes are bonded to another material that gives the planter its substance. Designed to resist corrosion, discoloration and water marks, the finishes include polished brass, aluminum and chrome.

Porcelain Planters: Steel planters that have been treated with a durable porcelain finish are available in lightweight models featuring "wet-looking" colors. They are virtually maintenance-free, and can be planted indirectly. The expanding field of applying spray finishes to planters means that more colors and more textures are continually put on the market.

Two Featherock planters show how pumice, a stone-like material soft enough to permit carving of openings for plants, can be attractively used for a planter. (Featherock, Inc.)

Redwood planters are commonly found in classic styles. These models show more unusual forms for the same material. (Heath Manufacturing Co.)

A desk-top metal drum planter comes in various finishes, including polished chrome, matte black or white, and satin bronze. (Architectural Supplements Inc.)

This hanging metal bowl planter is available in several sizes and finishes. (Architectural Supplements Inc.)

Available in transparent clear and transparent bronze, this drum planter makes it possible to watch a plant's roots develop. (Architectural Supplements Inc.)

Baskets used as planters help round off the corner of a room. (Chris Maynard)

A hanging plastic cube planter, this one comes in finishes of white plastic, transparent clear and transparent bronze. (Architectural Supplements Inc.)

Copper planters are available in many different shapes and sizes. They fit well into a colonial decor, and can be used on patios and balconies. (Riekes-Crisa Corp.)

Clay planters have taken on new shapes. (Bennington Potters) ▶
▼

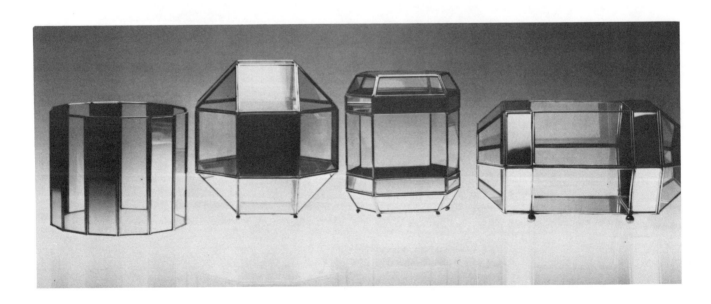

Models of hanging glass planters with mirrored sides include many striking designs. (Riekes-Crisa Corp.)

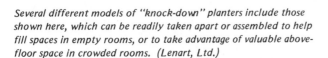

Several different models of "knock-down" planters include those shown here, which can be readily taken apart or assembled to help fill spaces in empty rooms, or to take advantage of valuable above-floor space in crowded rooms. (Lenart, Ltd.)

Transparent Planters: Watertight, transparent planters made from lucite and other plastics are another new development in container manufacturing. These make interesting attention-getters, since they enable you to see a plant's roots and the way they grow under the soil. See-through planters are made with and without seams, in a variety of geometric shapes.

Modular Planters: A unique new design idea offers modular-unit planters. Taken individually, each unit can hold a plant. If you choose, you can put together five or 50 units and have a uniform effect.

Modular planters are available as cubes or as round planters with squared-off tops.

Tile Planters: As hand-painted tiles become increasingly more popular in this country, so do planters made from the tiles. Kits including five uniform square tiles can be purchased specifically for planter construction, or you can make your own from squares you select yourself at a tile shop.

Basket Planters: Some of the newest planter designs look back to the age-old basket. They are made from such materials as woven willow strips, wicker

and steam-bent wood. Many come with attached casters and movable bases. Baskets are sold in many shops, and with a little imagination you can take one not specifically designed as a planter and turn it into one.
Copper Planters: Although copper is an expensive metal, cherished by many antique collectors, copper planters form a special part of the planter industry. Pounded into various shapes and sizes, copper-finished planters can create an interesting effect, especially in homes with colonial decor.
Novelty Planters: Increasing as a marketable item is a wide range of novelty planters to be used for the same purposes as more seriously designed planters. These should be used sparingly! Remember that an essential rule in planter decorating is never to let the planter outperform the plant in attracting attention. Novelty planters are available in many sizes and are made in the shapes of animals, hands, faces, hats, shoes and hundreds of other items.
Clay Planters: In addition to the classic styles of clay pots that can be found almost anywhere, a number of companies currently manufacture contemporary de-

signs from clay. These include fluted and ribbed textures, as well as smooth shapes suited for use alone, or with detachable stands and hangers.

Glass and Mirrored Planters: One of the newest uses of glass in planters is the design of many-faceted containers that reflect any available light in a room. Often glass planters include sides made from mirrors, in models that sit on table tops or hang from chains.

Plant Stands: There is nothing new about stands to hold planters, but some of the models currently available utilize new designs and materials, plus the convenience of being readily disassembled. These include various models of plant ladders and shelf units for use with pots and other display items.

A mixture of double petunias turns a window box into a brightly-colored garden. This variety is particularly well suited to withstand rainfall. (Courtesy Pan-American Seed Company)

Artificial lights are carefully concealed in this wooden shelf planter that could fit gracefully in any room. (Courtesy W. Atlee Burpee Company)

Hanging planters are suited to many different varieties of plants: this one made of clay holds an herb garden. (Courtesy W. Atlee Burpee Company)

An "environmental wall" combining concrete patterns with natural plants. These pockets hold soil for planting. The wall was cast using the Sculpcrete process. (Reproduced from Humanizing Concrete, Paul Ritter, PEER Institute Press, Perth, Western Australia, Austrialia, 1976)

Three logs and a kettle make a colonial planter; this tripod supports a geranium, one of the best and showiest container plants. (Photo by George Taloumis)

A cylindrical redwood planter is supported and held off the ground by unobtrusive angular legs. A bed of stones makes an excellent floor in a shady area. (Courtesy Rosenwach, Inc.)

Retired from service, a wheelbarrow has yet another use as a lawn planter, and a portable one at that. (Photo by George Taloumis)

A plant stand with removeable trays makes it possible to raise flowering plants in rooms that would not otherwise receive adequate light. (W. Atlee Burpee Company)

Curly cress grows from a window planter kit, a delightful means for harvesting your own herbs indoors. (Courtesy W. Atlee Burpee Company.)

A "Tumblin Tom" tomato flourishes and bears fruit in a hanging basket, proving that vegetables can be grown in only a few square feet of a sunny area. (Courtesy Ball Seed Company)

A simple wooden planter installed between the kitchen sink and window provides room for an attractive indoor garden. Notice how white stones are used to fill in around individual planters to give a finished appearance. (Courtesy Gerber Plumbing Fixtures Corporation)

Simple wooden crate planters hold tomatoes, an easily-grown container vegetable. (Photo by George Taloumis)

Humidity from showers and baths makes a bathroom an ideal place for planters. Notice how the mirror creates an illusion of plants on two sides of the room. (Courtesy Gerber Plumbing Fixtures Corporation)

*The several types of planters here are attractive additions to this
pool area. (Dean Development Co.)*

This wooden planter was built to camouflage a protruding brick corner wall. (Courtesy Rosenwach, Inc..)

Cylindrical ceramic planters are supported on redwood bases. Stones used around the base of the plants at soil level help retain moisture, especially on hot summer days. (Courtesy Group Artec)

Water lillies proliferate in a circular redwood planter, this one reinforced with galvanized steel bands at top and bottom. (Courtesy
Rosenwach, Inc.)

A cylindrical redwood planter helps eliminate the angular feeling of
a corner. Note how the color of the plant's leaves complements the
color of the brick wall. (Courtesy Rosenwach, Inc.)

Raised bed gardens, made from 1-inch by 6-inch weather-treated wood, provide good drainage and excellent productivity.

First, check to see that you have proper depth of good soil. The planters shown used supports for climbing plants such as cucumbers, peas; the support frames also deter traffic through the garden area. Other advantages of these raised beds are: they can be easily maintained from all sides; are extremely cost-efficient for the space occupied; allow the soil to be worked early in the season; adapt well to an already-set-up formal yard or garden; can be converted to cold frames for an extended growing season.

To construct, make boxes 4-feet by 6-feet or larger— up to 6-feet by 8-feet is manageable. Paths between boxes should be large enough to accommodate the width of a lawn mower (and garden cart or wheelbarrow, if desired), and should allow for a border planting of marigolds surrounding each box. The marigolds will repel many garden pests, as well as add to the appearance of the garden. (Photos courtesy of Patrick Mullaly, graphic designer, Ann Arbor, Mich.)

These two planters are examples of everyday items that can be recycled with only a coat of paint involved. In the foreground, a tub from a gas station used to check tires for leaks. In the background, a common metal barrel. (Photo by Chris Maynard)

Modular planters can stand alone, or be used in groups for a uniform-ly-designed effect. (Courtesy Bennington Potters)

This horizontal redwood cylinder, supported off the ground by sturdy legs, makes it possible to grow a pine tree on a patio. (Courtesy Rosenwach, Inc.)

Planters provide cheerful accents in a brightly-lit kitchen. Note how many different kinds are used—hanging planters, a floor planter, and a window planter in the breakfast nook—all without sacrificing floor space. (Photo by the makers of Armstrong resilient flooring)

Some planters, such as this rounded bowl-shaped style, can be filled with flowering annuals and moved back and forth between the indoors and the outdoors as the weather dictates. (Courtesy Group Artec)

This large urn, perhaps formerly used as a birdbath, becomes a stately planter when filled with geraniums. (Photo by George Taloumis)

Window planter filled with spring bulbs rests on overhanging window ledge. (Photo by George Taloumis)

A repainted antique carriage becomes a planter that would stop traffic! (Photo by George Taloumis)

Planter box built from stones on concrete footing can be made from three to six courses of brick or stone to enhance a garden area. (Courtesy Sakrete)

Multi-layer gardening is offered by a pyramid-style redwood planter that can hold many different kinds of flowering plants. (Courtesy Rosenwach, Inc.)

A cylindrical staved redwood planter rounds off a corner area. The plant in this photo appears dwarfed by the height of its container, but it may soon grow to proportionate size. (Courtesy Rosenwach, Inc.)

9

Suggested Plants
for Use in
Planters

Your choice of what to grow in planters, indoors or out, depends on your budget, your personal whims, and an understanding of what you intend growing plants to do for your home.

You can make some assumption before selecting your plants:

1. Flowering plants are more difficult to raise indoors than nonflowering plants.

2. Tropical plants or exotic varieties will need more attention in northern climates and during months when the outdoor temperatures drop and the heat is turned on.

3. All plants have fundamental requirements concerning light, moisture and humidity. You can stretch some of the basic rules for any plant and be rewarded with satisfactory growth, but your plant will be the first to tell you when its needs are not being met. Watch for warning signs and know how to correct them.

Many varieties of house plants and flowering annuals have been developed for home gardeners to raise from seeds—an economical and satisfying way to begin a planter garden. If you do not have the time, or if you want to install a planter and a 5-foot tree in your living room on a weekend, garden supply houses and greenhouses can fulfill your needs. A list of companies that specialize in mail order sales of seeds and plants is provided at the end of this book. Consult those of your choice to learn more about specific varieties, and to discover how many different plants are currently available for growing in window boxes, hanging baskets or large-sized planters.

SUGGESTED PLANTS FOR INDOOR PLANTERS

Books on house plants line shelves in almost any bookstore, and we will not attempt to provide you with a complete education in the subject. The following plants are included as suggestions in selecting stocks for your home planters.

African Violet

Popular in indoor window boxes on windowsills, or under artificial lights, African violets do not thrive in cool temperatures and should be kept warm and away from cool drafts. Some gardeners place planters for African violets directly on radiators or heating vents; if you do this, make sure the soil does not become too dry. Well cared-for plants will grow to a height of 4 to 6 inches and will continue to bloom throughout the year. East, west or north windows provide adequate light, but a southern exposure requires slight shading so that the leaves will not be burned. Keep soil regularly moist, and keep air humid, but avoid letting water come in direct contact with the leaves; this will cause spotting and rust marks.

Aloe

A tropical succulent plant, aloe has medicinal qualities and an opened leaf is said to ease the sting of a burn or a cut if applied to the broken skin. The plant thrives in sandy soil and will do extremely well in a planter that is placed in a sunny, warm bathroom window. If given good drainage and full sunlight for at least 6 hours, aloe can reach a height of 3 feet indoors.

Aluminum Plant

This low-growing plant has pointed leaves with silvery-white streaks and marks. It can be grown well under artificial light, or in a planter that is placed in bright, indirect light. Soil should be kept moderately moist. As plants reach a height of 8 inches or more, they can be successfully grown in a hanging planter from which they will trail down.

Many shapes and sizes of succulents and cacti are well suited to planter gardening. They require warm, dry climates, and careful use of water so their roots will not rot. (Chris Maynard)

*Ferns and an assortment of wild flowers, including trillium, grow in
an unusual step planter. (Chris Maynard)*

Flowering plants, leafy plants, and trailing plants can be combined in planters to provide attention-getting gardens. (BEH Housewares Corp.)

The wandering jew is a trailing plant that can be used in hanging baskets, or to adorn a window sill. (Photo by the makers of Armstrong interior furnishings)

Trailing peperomia lends accent to a hanging planter. (Chris Maynard)

Anthurium

An easy plant to grow in any exposure, anthurium can reach a height of 2 or 3 feet. It bears striking, heart-shaped leaves with red stems. Let soil dry out between watering but wash or mist leaves frequently to keep them at their most attractive.

Aphelandra

Also called Zebra Plant, aphelandra bears shiny leaves marked by bold white veins. A single yellow flower appears at the very top of the plant, if it has been given ideal conditions. Grow in good sunlight, but avoid the strong rays in a south window that may burn the leaves. Keep soil moderately moist at all times, and let the roots grow to be slightly pot bound before transplanting.

Aucuba

Another name for this plant is the gold dust tree, so given since the leaves have yellow specks on them.

Aucuba grows as high as 4 feet if given filtered sunlight, high humidity, and a moderate temperature drop at night.

Avocado

This is one of the most economical plants to grow, since you can start your own from a seed taken from a supermarket avocado. Wash the seed carefully after you have opened the fruit. Plant it directly in the soil, flat top down, so that approximately an inch is showing above the surface. Or, insert 4 toothpicks evenly spaced around the diameter, and suspend the pit in a glass of water. With either method, make sure there is adequate water so the seed does not dry out. Keep it away from sunlight until you can see other shoots appearing at the top or roots at the bottom. Place the seed in a sunny window—plant it in soil if you have started it in water—and watch a tall tree grow before your very eyes. Pinch back the highest growth to keep avocado plants bushy. Mist the leaves frequently and make sure they receive good light, or some direct sun.

Azalea

Ranging from small house plants that reach several feet to large shrubs that extend to many more feet, azaleas are known for their delightful flowers, in various shades of pink and white. This plant prefers acid soil, and will not perform well if its growing medium is not to its liking. The best location is a cool, sunny room that has a slight temperature drop at night. Some of the loveliest azaleas are those that gardeners regularly take with them into their morning showers. You may not want to go this far, but do plan to mist the plant regularly, and avoid dry climates. Many varieties can be taken outdoors in the spring after danger of frost has passed.

Beaucarnea

Known also as the elephant foot tree, beaucarnea can reach as high as a ceiling if it encounters ideal growing conditions. One or more trunks grow out of a swollen, wrinkled bark base that resembles an elephant's foot. Four or more hours of direct sunlight or a day of bright, indirect light are best for this tree. Let soil dry out between waterings and repot at the first sign of crowding in its pot. Such trees make good patio plants, and can be brought indoors in winter.

Boxwood

An outdoor evergreen, boxwood grows well in patios, or in smaller form in terrariums and bottle gardens. If planted in a row of outdoor planters, it will provide dense foliage and excellent privacy. Keep it away from direct sun; indoors give it bright, indirect sunlight and keep the room where it grows relatively cool.

Cactus

Along with succulents, the cactus family includes many different varieties of plants that are native to desert climates. (Cacti have spines; succulents have fleshy leaves. This is one basic way to distinguish between the two.) Keep cactus in sandy soil that drains well and let soil dry out well between waterings. Some cacti will reach a height of many feet indoors. It is not recommended that you leave them outdoors to encounter possible wet weather.

Caladium

Colorful arrow-shaped or spearhead leaves in shades of red, pink and green grow on this plant, which reaches a height of several feet. Keep caladium out of drafts, in warm rooms with indirect light or filtered sunlight. If exposed to full sun, the leaves will lose their color. Caladium requires a rest period each year for best results. Let soil become completely dry until the leaves wither. Let it sit in a cool, but not cold place for a few months; then repot, and bring the plant back to the light again. Water as before and watch new growth appear.

Camellia

This lovely flowering plant which bears red, white or pink waxy blooms can reach three feet in height. It does best in south or west light, in rooms that are relatively cool. Let soil dry out between waterings. Camellia is an excellent shrub for a patio. Bring it outdoors after all danger of frost has passed.

Cast-iron Plant

Reaching as much as three feet in height, this plant is so named for its hardiness, and the fact that it will do well in most exposures, including northern. Leaves can be as long as 30 inches, and 3 or 4 inches in width. Keep soil barely moist at all times.

Chinese Evergreen

Bearing shiny, green leaves, Chinese evergreen does well in poor light and dry climates. It will grow to be several feet tall. Let soil dry out between waterings, but for best results frequently wash the plant's leaves with a sponge, or mist them with warm water.

Citrus Trees

Ornamental varieties of kumquats, oranges and lemons can be grown indoors in planters that are given bright, sunny exposures. The best conditions for flowering and bearing fruit provide citrus plants with cool nights and high humidity. If your climate is dry, mist the plant frequently.

Corn Plant

A variety of dracona, corn plant resembles the native corn that is commonly grown in the garden. It does well in all exposures and climates. Leaves will fare best if they are frequently dusted and washed with a damp sponge.

Croton

Croton produces unusual colored leaves, in shades of copper, yellow, red and brown, that can reach a length of 18 inches, and a width of 6 inches. Striking accents to white walls or muted decor, this plant requires several hours of good sunlight daily, and it prefers a warm room to a cool one.

Cycad

A member of the succulent family, cycad has a palm-like appearance, and anyone who has grown it will tell you that it seems to thrive on neglect! This is an excellent choice for the urban gardener with little time to devote to indoor plants. Cycad is resistant to cold, and is blessedly hardy to most indoor plant diseases. Grow it in any exposure.

Cyclamen

The large red or white flowers that a cyclamen bears are so fragrant that their oil is available as a perfume. A well cared-for plant will reach a height of several feet. Ideal conditions are cool nights and good light during the day; east, west or south windows are suitable. Mist the plant daily, water frequently, and be sure there is adequate drainage to avoid root rot. Where possible, water from below.

Dracena

Dracenas encompass many varieties of plants, some very different from others. They include those with narrow pointed leaves, and those with more rounded shapes. All dracenas respond to bright indirect light, and will do well in northern windows. Keep soil moist, but do not be as concerned about misting, since these plants can handle dry climates.

Dumb Cane

This plant is so named not for its appearance, but for the fact that if the leaves are eaten, they will render a person speechless for as long as an hour. Both the leaves and the stems are poisonous, and should be carefully kept from pets and small children. Dumb cane has large leaves with white stripes and will reach a height

of 5 feet. To keep it shorter, cut it back from the top. It will do well in even the dimmest light, but let the soil dry out between waterings. Too much water will cause roots and stems to rot.

Fatsia

Fatsia looks as if it might be a distant cousin of the maple tree; its leaves form the same pattern, but grow to be as large as 16 inches across. A mature plant can reach 6 feet tall. Keep fatsia in east or west light, in a relatively cool room. Keep soil moist, and fertilize as often as once a month to keep the plant healthy.

Fig

This large group of plants includes weeping fig, with shiny, pointed leaves, and the popular rubber plant, with large rounded leaves. Figs do well in bright indirect light, but should not be exposed to direct sunlight. Keep soil barely moist.

Gardenia

A white flower frequently worn as a corsage on formal occasions, gardenia has a distinctive fragrance. It should be grown in full sun, where a healthy plant will produce many shiny dark green leaves and waxy blossoms. Let the room your plant is in cool off at night, keep the soil moist and mist frequently. If the leaves turn yellow, fertilize the plant more frequently.

Geranium

Popular in window boxes and patio tubs, geranium will flower throughout the year if kept in a brightly-lit room. It prefers clay soil, and will not flower if the growing medium contains too much nitrogen. Let soil dry out between waterings. Yellow leaves can indicate too much water, or pockets of pooling water beneath the soil line. If you plant geranium outdoors in summer, bring it into the house and keep it growing all winter. If you pinch back the branches, you can turn an ordinary plant into a tree that will live for many years.

Hibiscus

Hibiscus is the state flower of Hawaii, and its beautiful large pink or red flowers will stop traffic in your home. It prefers full sun, and should be misted frequently. Where climates are mild, hibiscus can be grown outdoors all year; in colder areas you can put it out in summer and bring it indoors in the fall. Let soil dry out between waterings, except when the plant is in flower; then keep it well watered.

Jade Plant

This succulent has rounded leaves and can mature through a period of years to be several feet tall. The older the plant, the more fragile are its leaves. Handle a developed jade very carefully. Ideal conditions provide four to six hours of sunlight daily, but the plant will also thrive in bright, constant daylight. Let soil dry out between waterings; rotted, black leaves will be the jade's way of telling you that you are overwatering.

Jerusalem Cherry

Capable of growing to a height of 3 or 4 feet, this ornamental fruit tree likes full sun, but will grow satisfactorily in bright light. It produces white flowers followed by a profusion of red berries; the berries are poisonous, so keep the plant away from pets and small children. Let soil become slightly dry between waterings, but don't let the plant wither.

Laurel

This plant is the source of bay leaves, so prized in cooking. It requires direct sun for 4 or 5 hours daily, or will grow to bright, indirect light. Keep soil barely moist at all times.

Norfolk Island Pine

Resembling a tiny Christmas tree, Norfolk pine can grow 3 to 6 inches per year, and is capable of reaching a height of several feet indoors. Outdoors, in suitable climates, it will grow much taller. Plant in bright indirect light, in an east or west exposure; some bright northern light is also suitable. Keep soil barely moist and avoid overwatering.

Orchid

Many varieties of orchids can be raised indoors. They prefer cool areas, and an east or west window. Let soil dry out between waterings, but mist flowers and leaves daily. If you are interested seriously in orchid culture, send for a catalogue on these exotic plants, and carefully study the requirements for their growing medium and care.

Palms

There are hundreds of different palms, all highly ornamental plants that grow from 12 inches to many feet tall. Most will thrive in northern light, but they should be shielded from direct sunlight. Keep them warm, and in a slightly acid soil. Keep soil from drying out, but don't let it get soaked at any time. Wash the leaves of larger palms with a damp sponge.

Peperomia

Peperomia is available in many varieties, including plants that trail, and those with variegated leaves. Grow them in bright light of an east or west window; they will also grow fairly well in northern exposures. Let soil dry out between waterings, and spray frequently to maintain humidity level.

Piggyback Plant

This unusual looking plant, sometimes called Mother of Thousands, produces new leaves from the bases of older leaves; thus, it looks as if new growth is getting a free ride. The leaves, covered with a thin, fuzzy layer, are susceptible to collecting dust. Mist them frequently or give them a bath with the hose attachment in a kitchen sink. Let soil dry out between waterings. Start new plants by rooting leaves in soil.

Pittosporum

An attractive larger plant that can grow to be 6 feet tall, pittosporum has oval-shaped, shiny leaves. It does best in bright, indirect light, or in places that will provide a few hours of direct sun daily. Keep soil on the dry side, and prune the plant to keep it shapely.

Schefflera

Also called umbrella tree, this popular large plant can get as high as 8 feet tall. Its leaves are borne in large, glossy groups of 5 at the end of a long stem. Schefflera grows well in bright, indirect light. Mist it frequently and be sure to wash the leaves with a damp sponge at least once a month to keep them from getting clogged by dust and dirt.

Snake Plant

Commonly found in combination arrangements in planters of all sizes, the snake plant is a long-standing member of a group of house plants that are almost impossible to neglect. Growth is satisfactory in any exposure, with little water. If moved into southern light, snake plants sometimes will flower. It lives for many years, and can grow to a height of 30 inches.

Spathiphyllum

Shiny, large, green, pointed leaves and outstanding white flowers make this plant an interesting one to grow. Keep it away from direct sun in a warm room. Let soil remain moist at all times.

Spleenwort

A typical plant of this variety has leaves that grow to be 15 inches long; other smaller varieties include the bird's nest fern and species that are well suited to terrarium planters. They can stand dry air, but their soil should be kept moist.

Swiss Cheese Plant

This plant is sometimes confused with philodendron, but it is not related. Actually a vine native to Mexico and Guatemala, Swiss cheese plant gets its name from the perforations that appear in each of its 12-inch leaves. It does well in bright, indirect light, and can get as tall as a ceiling in just a few years; cut it back at the top to keep it smaller. Soil should be barely moist, but soak through with each watering. Wash leaves frequently to keep them clean.

PLANTS FOR HANGING PLANTERS

Some plants flourish in either ground or window planters, as well as in hanging baskets and pots. But true hanging plants will not do their best unless their leaves are touching nothing but air. Perhaps they feel crowded when they make contact with solid objects. The following is a list of some of the more popular hanging plants for indoor gardens. Some can be moved outdoors for the summer, or to get an extra boost from a sunny day.

Asparagus Fern

Feathery, needle-like leaves and branches give this plant its name, and if you have ever seen asparagus growing in a garden, you'll understand why. Best suited to an east or west window, it should be allowed to dry out between waterings. Mist often.

Mixed color marigolds can be successfully grown in window boxes, and are good cut flowers for indoor arrangements. (Burpee Seeds)

Begonia

There are many different varieties of begonias, and most are suited to hanging baskets. They include three main groups: tuberous, rhizomatous and fibrous. When planted in wire baskets or hanging planters, begonias will put on a dramatic show of color. They can be grown outdoors in summer and brought indoors for continued bloom in winter. Place them in indirect light or filtered sunlight, and keep soil barely moist. Pinch the plants back after they have flowered to discourage legginess.

Bougainvillea

A tropical plant, this one has stunning red flowers and branches that can trail, or climb. It should be trimmed to keep it flowering. Bougainvillea prefers cool rooms and bright light, such as that of a west window. Soil should remain moist at all times. If you choose to summer this plant outdoors, carefully protect it from the sun's direct rays.

Columnea

Also available as a bushy pot plant, columnea is a delightful hanging plant, which produces striking orange or yellow flowers. It enjoys a sunny or bright window, and frequent watering and misting.

Donkey-tail Sedum

A succulent, this plant has unusual, thick leaves that grow so closely together it is impossible to see any stem at all. Indeed, the plant looks almost as though it were braided. It can reach a length of several feet, but the older the plant, the more fragile it is; fertilize old plants well, and keep them out of high traffic areas. They prefer full sun, but will tolerate good light.

Ferns

Available in many varieties, ferns make good hanging plants, especially for designs that call for a repeated use of the same plant. They can support fronds that reach 3 feet in length. The soil should be kept barely moist. Hang the plants in bright, indirect light.

Fuchsia

Noted for its dramatic, tear-shaped pink, rose and purple flowers, fuchsia does well on patios, in doorways or in a bright window. It should not receive full sun, but does require good air circulation to keep it flowering. Let soil dry out in winter, and be on guard for infestations of white spider mite, a problem this plant must frequently overcome.

Inch Plant

Sporting large, pointed leaves with white stripes, inch plant resembles wandering Jew. It likes sunny windows, but will do nicely in east or west light. Keep soil on the dry side, and pinch the plant back frequently to avoid stringiness. Root new plants from cuttings.

Lipstick Plant

Green, waxy leaves and striking red tubular flowers characterize this plant, which prefers warm and humid climates. Fertilize it every 3 or 4 weeks, and cut it back after it has flowered. Give it bright light, and mist often.

Miniature Roses

Delightful flowering plants for a hanging basket, miniature roses should have good light and moist soil to grow well. They thrive under artificial lights, if given 12 to 16 hours of light per day beneath a several tube fixture. Keep them in the sun and be sure the soil is on the acid side. If you repot them, keep them cool until their new roots have had a chance to develop.

Philodendron

An old standby for people who say they can't grow house plants, this one is very easy to grow well. Encompassing several hundred species, it is a good climber, and likes to have something to grab onto; some varieties will also do nicely in hanging planters. Give them bright, indirect light and keep soil from completely drying out. In areas where only dim light is available, philodendron will grow, but their new leaves will be smaller than the older ones.

Pothos

Pothos looks like a variegated philodendron, but is not of the same group. It does well in dim light and dry climates. Let soil dry out between waterings and wash and mist leaves frequently to keep them shiny.

Spider Plant

Members of the lily family, spider plants are so named because they produce new plants that look like spiders at the ends of long runners or stems. They have striking green and white striped leaves, and do well in bright, indirect light. Fertilize often, and keep the soil from drying out between waterings.

Wandering Jew

Variegated green and white or purple and green leaves grow quickly on this plant and make it a good one to use where you wish to have rapid growth. Keep it in bright, indirect light, and let the soil dry out between waterings.

Marigolds constitute an all-around favorite, whether grown in patio boxes, window planters, or tubs and barrels. (Burpee Seeds)

FLOWERING PLANTS FOR OUTDOOR PLANTERS

Many lovely flowering plants that can be grown on patios, balconies and in window boxes are economical to start from seed. Consult seed catalogues for the differences between the many names that are currently available. Here are some of the easiest and most rewarding to grow.

Ageratum

Well suited to a window box or rock garden, ageratum has white, blue and purple flowers that reach as tall as a foot. It does well in full sun or partial shade, and can be brought indoors at the end of the summer. Plants 5 to 6 inches high will spread to a foot across.

Alyssum

Forming a carpet of flowers, this plant's blossoms are white, pink or purple. It reaches only 4 inches in height, but can spread to be 12 inches across. It is attractive when planted on the topsoil of a large tree planter. Sow seeds directly on the ground after the last frost.

Browallia

A rare color, true blue, makes this plant's bell-shaped flowers a lovely addition to many a garden. It does well in areas that receive partial shade, and will bloom indoors as well as out. It can reach a height of 18 inches, but plants that are expected to grow this tall outdoors should be started indoors in the spring.

Calendula

An easy to grow plant with yellow and orange flowers, calendula does best in full sun or partial shade. The largest flowers are 4 1/2 to 5 inches across, and are borne on plants that reach a height of 2 to 2 1/2 feet. They make excellent cut flowers. Sow seed directly on the soil, after all danger of frost has passed.

Celosia

Rich, red flowers with a feathery bloom, or crested flowers with an appearance of ruffled velvet, celosia is a very bright ornamental plant, striking when used with white flowering plants in the same planter. Plants will reach a height of 6 to 8 inches. Start seeds indoors in the spring, or sow directly on soil after frost danger has passed.

Coleus

A plant with colored foliage, and shades of red, pink and green, coleus prefers partial shade, and can successfully be grown indoors or out. Strong sun will bleach the colors out of the leaves. Plants reach a height of 15 inches, but should be pinched back to keep them shapely.

Dianthus

Reaching a height of 18 inches, this plant has small white, pink or red flowers that from a distance resemble carnations. The foliage is a grey-blue color. Dianthus prefers full sun or slight shade. Sow seeds directly into pots.

Nasturtiums grow and flower in a standing planter box, providing bright color in even a small garden space. (Massachusetts Horticultural Society)

Impatiens

Brightly colored flowers in shades of red, white, or pink bloom on this plant, which has fleshy stems. It blooms year round, and can be grown indoors or out. Keep it in partial shade and hang older plants, pinching them back to keep them bushy.

Marigold

Some people do not care for the odor of marigold, a distinct, somewhat pungent fragrance. It provides lovely yellow and orange flowers, easy to grow in areas that receive full sun. Marigold is available in many varieties, ranging from 6 to 40 inches tall at maturity. Use dwarf varieties in flower boxes.

Nasturtium

A good outdoor hanging plant, nasturtium reaches several feet in length when grown in full sun. It produces red, orange or yellow flowers, all excellent, bright colors. Let soil dry out between waterings.

Nicotiana

Preferring sun or some shade, this plant has red, purple or white flowers that remain open only in the morning and late afternoon; hot sun and heat cause them to close up. The blooms make good cut flowers, and the plant ranges from 8 to 40 inches tall.

Pansy

An old favorite in window boxes and rock gardens, pansy is primarily blue, purple and yellow with distinctive faces on each flower. It grows well in full sun or partial shade. For the best results, pinch the flowers off regularly to make room for new ones.

Petunia

Available as single or double flowers, petunia comes in bright shades of red, pink, purple and white, some with stripes. It is easy to grow in sunny locations, and flowers that are well cared for will reach 3 to 5 inches in width. Double petunia is especially attractive in hanging baskets.

Phlox

This plant produces a profusion of blue, violet, pink or white flowers that like full sun. It grows to be 6 to 15

Snapdragons lend soft colors to any planter garden, and double as attractive cut flowers for indoor arrangements. (Burpee Seeds)

inches tall, and is well suited to cut flower arrangements.

Portulaca

Portulaca has yellow, white, red, pink or purple flowers that grow on fleshy, short stems. It does well in hanging planters, in full sun, where it can trail down to a foot or more. Keep soil on the dry side.

Salvia

Most commonly associated with flaming red spike flowers, salvia also is available in pink and blue varieties. It prefers sun or partial shade, and reaches a height of 8 to 30 inches.

Snapdragon

Another good cut flower, snapdragon blooms grow at the end of tall spikes, and each tiny petal resembles a dragon's head. Colors include pink, red, yellow and lavender. The plant grows from 6 to 40 inches high. Dwarf varieties are excellent for window boxes and small planters. Grow in full sun.

Verbena

Most commonly planted for patriotic red, white and blue gardens, verbena has bright colors. Flowers reach from 4 to 10 inches in height and grow on bushy plants that spread rapidly. It prefers full sun, but will tolerate moderate shade.

Zinnia

Bright flowers in pink, red, orange and yellow grow on plants that range in height from 6 to 32 inches. Most flowers have layers of petals, but some single varieties are sold. When planted in partial shade, zinnia sometimes grows taller, trying to reach the sun.

Outdoor Planters

With only a little extra attention to the many varieties of plants suited to container culture, you can design a planter garden that is continually in flower during your growing season.

Take, for example, a planter that is 3 feet long and 1 foot wide. Even an area this small can support many different choices. First, in the early spring, set in tulip bulbs or a mixture of other flowering bulbs, which have been wintered in pots in a cold frame or have been forced indoors, to a depth of approximately 4 inches. After these have flowered, and when they have begun to wither, trim off the tops and let the rest of the growth dry up on its own. Plant a row of pansies which will flower for several weeks, all around the perimeter of the box to conceal the last signs of the bulbs' leaves, and then sow one layer, in alternating spots, of annuals, such as marigolds, cosmos, bachelor buttons or asters. None of these varieties will affect the dormant bulbs, since their roots can coexist in the same area.

Consult seed catalogues for further suggestions on the flowering times of various plants and for additional information on choosing selections that will flower throughout the summer and complement each other in your planter.

10

Planter Problems

Many reasons underlie plant failure. Neglect, a sudden change in temperature, or an infestation of pests can make a healthy plant send out danger signals in a matter of hours.

Each problem is different, and only you can detect the exact cause. But if you have paid careful attention to the requirements of a well-functioning planter, then sudden changes can be traced to the plant itself rather than to its container.

PREVENTION

Consider the following suggestions to help prevent plant sickness:

1. Always use sterilized potting soil indoors, and make sure any stones or bricks that you bring indoors to use with your planters have also been sterilized. If you are not using commercially-prepared soil, place your own soil on a baking sheet and leave it in a 250 degree oven for two hours. Do the same thing with bricks and stones.

2. Mist and wash your plants' leaves frequently. Keep them free from dust and grime, and as unpolluted from city air as possible. Washing will also help remove any minuscule insects that may be hiding on the under sides of leaves.

3. When you bring a plant indoors after it has spent the summer outside, inspect it carefully for insects and worms. Always re-pot such a plant in sterilized soil when it comes indoors.

4. If you find a sick plant, immediately quarantine it and keep it away from healthy plants. Wash your hands after handling it, to avoid passing a disease along to healthy plants through touching them.

5. If you have been unable to save a plant, throw it away and get rid of the soil it has grown in. Do not keep a dead plant around to contaminate others you may have.

SPECIFIC PROBLEMS AND SOLUTIONS

Some of the most common planter problems are outlined below. These are not *all* the things that can happen to your plants, but they are the most common ailments.

Anthracnose Disease: This fungus problem causes spots on leaves and frequently makes the ends of the leaves turn dark brown or black. Too much moisture in the air, periods of unusual rains, or keeping a plant (that likes dry climates) in a bathroom or steamy kitchen—all can cause anthracnose disease. To cure the problem, keep all moisture at a minimum, remove affected leaves, and spray plant with a fungicide available at a garden supply store. The label will mention this disease by name and give instructions for its cure.

Discolored Leaves: Since a plant uses its leaves to gather moisture and to indicate sudden changes, complaints about house plants often revolve around discolored or yellowing leaves.

Most commonly, yellow leaves are the plant's way of saying that it is vitamin deficient, or that an insect pest is sucking away its moisture. In some cases, yellow leaves are also the result of too little water. Burned, browned leaves mean too much sun.

If you have not been paying attention to your plant's needs for fertilizer, purchase fish emulsion or some other type of commercially prepared nutrient and, following the directions, give your plant a shot of it. Remove all yellow leaves at the same time.

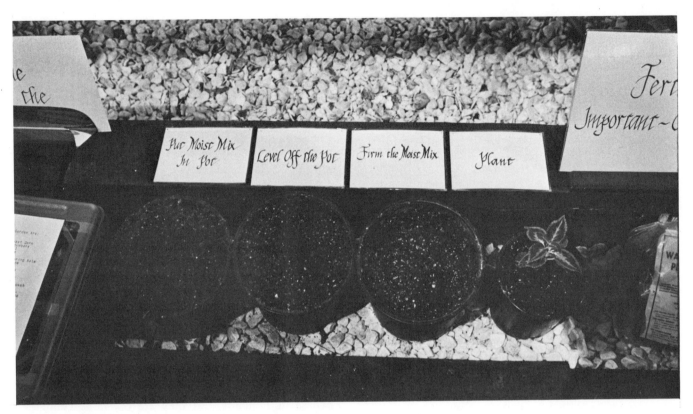

Some problems with planter gardening begin with improper planting of whatever you are trying to grow. This display reiterates an important first step in getting a plant started in a new environment. (Chris Maynard)

If you have been fertilizing, the problem could be mites or other insects (discussed in detail later in this chapter). Carefully inspect the leaves for any signs of them and treat well with an insecticide or a thorough shower of warm water. Remove affected plant to a cool place and continue to treat it until new growth resumes and no more yellow leaves appear.

Wilting and Stunted Growth: If your plants continue to look withered several hours after you have watered them, they could be responding to a lack of proper humidity, which also causes leaves to turn brown on the edges and can check all new growth. To solve this problem, install a humidifier or begin a program of misting plants daily. Keep room temperatures cool. Another solution is to place the affected plants on pebbles in a tray filled with water. Do not let the planters themselves touch the water, but allow about a half an inch of water to reach just to the top of the stones.

Pooling Water: Water that stands on top of your planter's soil after watering is a sign of compacted soil. If the spaces within the soil are pressed tightly together, there is inadequate aeration and root systems may be suffering from lack of air. Clay soil is the chief offender. Remove the plant from the planter and add peat moss, vermiculite or sand to the soil.

Also check to make sure the planter has adequate drainage; if there is no opening in the bottom, remove the plant and stir the soil carefully. Replant in a pot that does have an opening, and set it inside the planter. Let the soil dry out before rewatering.

Insect Pests: A host of insects cause problems in house plants and a smart gardener is constantly on the alert for them. In general, insects thrive in hot, dry environments and attack plants that are near radiators and other heating elements.

Aphids are small, round insects that form clusters on a plant's leaves and stems. If allowed to propagate uncontrolled, they will suck the moisture from the plant and destroy it. Mealy bugs are waxy insects that also cluster on stems and branches. They do not look as much like insects as do aphids, and they move more slowly, but a careful eye will be able to spot them. Both secrete a sticky substance that you can feel. Red spider mite and other types of mites are the most difficult

This drooping avocado plant was not pruned sufficiently in its infancy. It also shows signs of limp leaves, possibly caused by being rootbound in too small a container. (Chris Maynard)

A Westinghouse research scientist shows how a plant grown under fluorescent lamps (left) is healthier than a plant of the same age and species that was grown under another light source. (Westinghouse Electric Corporation)

insects to discern, but they often leave signs of webs and crystallized coatings on the under sides of leaves.

Another destructive insect is the white fly, which looks like a tiny white moth. You can actually watch it fly off a leaf when you touch the edge. White flies gather in groups and slowly destroy leaf tissue.

For all four types of pest, try first washing the plant thoroughly with a spray of water, either from a kitchen hose or directly under a bathroom shower. Where possible, direct the water onto trouble spots, and force the bugs off with your fingers or a cotton swab.

If more bugs appear in a day, and they may very well do this since they also affect soil, purchase an insecti-cide from your nearest plant supply shop. Malathion has an unpleasant odor, but is one of the most effective chemicals. Follow the directions carefully, and keep on a routine program until your plant is cured.

Leaves that are actually chewed—that show ragged edges and signs of nibbling—have probably been at-tacked by a larger pest. Grasshoppers, cockroaches, and earwigs can all cause damage indoors as well as out-doors. They often hide at the base of planters or in safe places nearby and come out at night. Inspect leaves for any signs of them and soak the soil with a solution of malathion or another insecticide.

Insufficient Light: Major problems with growing plants frequently stem from inadequate amounts of light striking the leaves, resulting in unsatisfactory quanti-ties of energy.

Aside from common sense, and watching your plants for signs that they need more light—stems that become spindly and stringy and stretch toward what light is available, or yellow, withered leaves—two other systems have been designed to indicate whether or not a particular area in your home is adequately lighted for specific plants.

The first concerns itself with the standard measure of light, called a foot candle: very simply, this is the amount of light that a burning candle gives off at the distance of one foot. You can purchase a foot candle meter at a hardware store. Also, camera shops sell con-version charts which enable you to use a photographic

Plant stretching toward available light shows signs of leggy growth as its necessary light requirements are not met. (Chris Maynard)

Sav-a-Plant Moisture Meter works on a self-powered basis to show meter readings that correspond with a plant's moisture needs. (AMI Medical Electronics)

light meter for a reading that can be translated into foot candles. Enlist the aid of the light meter to determine available light in your home. Set it for a film speed of ASA 200, with the shutter speed at 1/50 of a second. Since a white wall will show reflected light (more than is actually present) and a dark wall will do the opposite, place a piece of gray cardbord behind the area where you wish to take the reading. Place the meter 30 inches from the floor, face pointing toward the ceiling, and gauge the light in your room. The following chart shows approximate translations of meter readings to foot candles.

For a listing of commonly found house plants and their required foot candles, check *Foliage House Plants* by James Crockett. (See appendix; check your local library for a copy.)

You can also check on your plant's light sources by using a small meter that you can place directly in the soil, manufactured by AMI Medical Electronics, New York, N.Y. It indicates available light and moisture by means of a needle moving against a colored background. A reference book that comes with the meter shows what the best readings should be, and what areas indicate danger signs.

Foot Candles	Light Meter Set For 200 ASA Film Speed, at 1/50 sec.
10	F1.4
50	F2.8
80	Midpoint F2.8-F4
100	F4
10	F1.4
30	F2
50	F2.8
30	F2
70	Midpoint F2.8-F4
50	F2.8
30	F2
50	F2.8
70	Midpoint F2.8-F4
30	F2
100	F4
200	F5.6
30	F2
70	Midpoint F2.8-F4
70	Midpoint F2.8-F4
30	F2
70	Midpoint F2.8-F4
150	Midpoint F4-F5.6
30	F2

11

Converting and Adapting Planters for Other Uses

Americans are the most mobile people on earth. We move from smaller apartments to bigger ones, from campuses to cottages, from the city to the country. In all these moves our space requirements are constantly changing. What was a suitable planter yesterday may be too big or too small today. By their very nature, planters are decorative accents for a variety of lifestyles, and we must be ready to adapt them to our ever-changing living spaces. Often, we must be prepared to discard those that no longer fit our current space or lifestyle.

But rather than merely discard, often we may convert planters into other useful items. Because while we are a mobile society, we are also a thrifty and ingenious one, and these virtues may be utilized in the act of transforming planters for other home and apartment uses. So, whether you suddenly decide that a particular planter has outlived its usefulness for raising plants, or you inherit a built-in planter when you purchase a house, here are some alternatives.

INSIDE
Storage Space

Unwanted wooden planters are especially well suited for storing household items, especially if they are built in. If the planter has suffered any damage, add a new bottom or side—whatever is required to put it into shape. Then clean it carefully and paint it with oil-based enamel. Depending on the size, you can store toys, athletic equipment, sewing items, Christmas tree ornaments and lights or small garden tools. Make an attractive top that fits on to it so you will have another surface to use. If, for example, you keep yarn or sewing items in the bottom, you can also place a light, an ashtray or a small growing plant on the top.

Tables

Round tub planters and wooden cubes can be readily converted into tables. Upend them, cut pieces of wood or glass to fit the bottoms, and use them at the ends of a couch, or use one as a coffee table. Two smaller upended planters can support a piece of wood several feet long and of the same width as the planters. Such a table can be used for house plants, for books, or for a stereo system.

Vases

Especially suited to dried flower arrangements, some taller planters also serve as containers to hold fall gourds and cut flowers. Be sure anything that holds water is not porous and that it will not leave a mark on the surface it touches.

Lamps

Glass terrarium planters and bottle gardens can readily be converted into dramatic lamps for use on a kitchen or living room table. With the garden intact (see page 20 for instructions on planting a terrarium garden), insert a lamp fixture with an attached cord and plug into the neck. The plants inside the bottle will thrive on the light from your lamp, and you will have created an interesting conversation piece.

Kitty Litter Boxes

Tray planters made of plastic or metal can be converted into containers for kitty litter. Make sure they can be easily cleaned and, if necessary, build on a second,

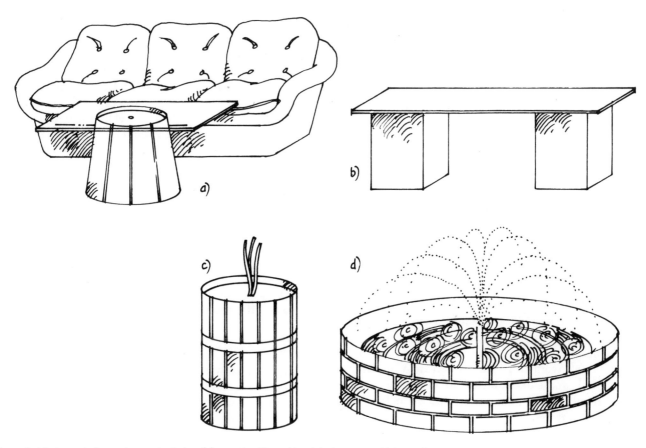

Several objects made from planters include: (a) round coffee table with glass top, which can function as a cocktail table or an end table, (b) rectangular low table, also useful as a coffee table or shelf for plants; (c) large patio candle with several wicks; and (d) a fountain.

higher edge. Metal planters should be lined with plastic to prevent rust or leakage at the seams from moisture.

Waste Baskets

Planters that have been used as the outside, decorative portion of other containers usually do not have openings in the bottom and can serve as waste baskets, if they are large enough. Baskets, ceramic pots and wooden barrels will all work well in this capacity. If the planter is not washable, line it with a plastic or paper bag to keep it clean.

Christmas Tree Stands

A planter such as a redwood tub makes an ideal support for the family Christmas tree. Place a small pail or watertight container inside it, and secure the tree by placing bricks or stones around its base, and piling

them up toward the top until the tree is stabilized. Fill the inner container with water.

Organizers for Individual Items

One of the cleverest uses for a planter is to convert it into a handy organizer. A woman who sews constantly has installed a metal planter box inside her sewing room cupboard as a file for patterns with each one put away according to number. This same idea can be applied to recipe cards, or household business records.

Lamp Shades

Plastic tubs and even clay pots can be converted into striking lamp shades. Fit them over an existing lamp, or thread an electrical fixture and cord through their bottom opening. An elaborate use of planters as shades can be accomplished by attaching several similar small planters to a large, multi-bulb fixture. If using plastic materials make sure they do not come in contact with bare bulbs, for many of the newer plastics are not resistant to heat.

Candles and Candle Holders

A planter without a drainage opening can be made into a dramatic candle. Select one or several wicks, depending on the width and depth of your planter, and secure them at the bases of the container. The wicks should extend at least six inches above the top of the planter; lay a stick or broom handle across the top of the planter and roll the ends of the wicks around it, to keep them centered and straight. Fill the planter with melted wax and let it harden. Unroll the wicks, trim them, and you have a candle that should burn for many hours.

If you don't want to go this far, create a holder by placing a tall candle inside a clay pot or upend the pot and secure a candle to its upturned end by melting the wax on the bottom.

OUTSIDE

Birdhouses

A smaller wooden planter can readily be made into a birdhouse. Simply add a side to the open top and, if they are not large enough, widen the drainage openings in the bottom. Suspend it from a tree by a piece of wire, or attach it to a metal pole that a cat cannot climb.

Bird Feeders

A standard hanging planter made from clay or plastic can serve as an excellent bird feeder. Suspend it from the porch or a nearby tree by strong wire. (Wire is better than string or rope, since it keeps the planter from swinging in the wind and frightening the birds.) Fill it with bird seed up to about an inch deep, and replenish as the supply goes down. A neglected planter hanging in a tree has, on occasion, been used by a bird as a modern-style nest. Should you ever discover that a nest has been built in such a planter, be sure to leave it undisturbed until the birds are finished with it.

Bird Baths

A large stone or concrete cemetery planter, or a bowl-shaped planter that can be supported on a pedestal, makes an excellent bird bath. If the bowl part of the planter will not hold water, you can either line it with a thin film of cement or find a bowl that will fit securely in place. (You may have to add a rock or a brick to the bottom of the bowl to keep it from tipping.) Fill with water and, if you wish, plant tall flowering plants all around it. Clean it frequently to avoid algae and scum.

Sand Boxes

Large, shallow wooden planters that have been installed in yard areas can be made into children's sand boxes. Reinforce the sides if they are not as high as 12 inches, and fill with clean sand. Make a covering so you can keep the sand dry during rain storms.

Compost Containers

A large tub planter, box or barrel that can be positioned with ready access to the house, but not close enough to give off unpleasant odors, can be used to create a compost pile. A metal or plastic barrel is ideal; make sure the inside of a wooden planter is well treated with moisture-resistant paint. Save only uncooked scraps from fruits and vegetables, and sprinkle soil on top from time to time to help break down the foods. A good measure is to cut a door or space near the bottom so you can scoop out the oldest, most broken-down matter.

Fountains

A securely-built brick or stone planter in your back yard might support a fountain. Line the inside with plastic or metal and build a tiered fountain, then landscape around the edges. Install a pump and other apparatus and enjoy a spectacular sight. If you want the fountain to work at night, be sure to include lights in your installation.

Rock Gardens

If you have a large, shallow outdoor planter that has been installed in such a way that removal is difficult, consider turning it into a rock garden. Fill it with fieldstones or round rocks arranged in random patterns. Such rocks in smaller sizes can also be used in a narrow trough planter. Fill in between the cracks with soil and scatter seeds on top. If you select plants particularly suited to rock garden culture, you'll find that your planter supports a lovely, small and ever-blooming garden.

Ash Trays

Airports and other public places frequently use urns full of sand as ashtrays, and you can follow this idea on your patio. A very large planter is a waste of space in this capacity, but a smaller one filled with sand can be a smokeless and tidy way to extinguish cigarettes outdoors. Be sure to plug up any drainage openings before filling the planter with sand, to avoid leakage when you pick it up.

Garden Benches

A built-in planter that is no longer needed can serve as a useful bench in a garden or patio. Cover the top with a length of plywood or other wood and attach a cushion made from weather-resistant fabric, such as plastic or canvas.

Barbecues

A long, narrow planter made of brick or stone can make an ideal barbecue. Line it with stones and then charcoal for an open fire. Lay a length of steel grating or wire across the top and you're ready for some cooking. If the dimensions are right, such a planter can also serve as the base for a small stove or hibachi that would leave a heat mark on the grass or on your patio.

APPENDIX

FURTHER READING

California Redwood Association
617 Montgomery Street
San Francisco, CA 94111
Free literature on redwood planters, ideas for their construction and use.

Cornell University
Department of Communication Arts
Research Park
Ithaca, NY 14853
Request copy of publications list. Publishes many booklets relating to planter gardening.

Time-Life Books
New York, NY 10020
Foliage House Plants by James Crockett, 1972. Includes foot-candle requirements for house plants, plus many tips on their care.

Gerber Plumbing Fixture Corp.
4656 West Touhy Avenue
Chicago, IL 60646
Gerber Bath Book, with ideas for installing planters in home bathrooms. $1.

Sakrete
P.O. Box 17087
Cincinnati, OH 42511
Instruction booklet for planters you can make at home.

University of California
Cooperative Extension
1422 South 10th Street
Richmond, CA 94804
Request copy of publications list. Publishes many booklets relating to planter gardening.

COMPANIES THAT MANUFACTURE OR SELL PLANTERS AND EQUIPMENT

Adam Jay, Inc.
340 Main Street
Worcester, MA 01608
Kangaroo Pouch Planters.

AMI Medical Electronics
116 East 27th Street
New York, NY 10016
"Sav-a-Plant" moisture meters.

Architectural Supplements
341–A East 62nd Street
New York, NY 10021
Contemporary design planters sold through designers and decorators.

L. S. Beck, Inc.
11 East 68th Street
New York, NY 10021
Lucite cube planters.

BEH Housewares Corp.
1150 Broadway
New York, NY 10001
Humidi-Tray Planters.

Bennington Potters
324 County Street
Bennington, VT 05201
Modular clay planters, cube planters, modern hanging planters.

Country Garden
2634 Ocean View Drive
Point Arena, CA 95468
Redwood pyramid planters.

Eagle Forest Products
P.O. Box 6550
Sacramento, CA 95860
Presto Planters in make-it-yourself kits.

Earthway Products, Inc.
P.O. Box 547
Bristol, IN 46507
Indoor garden center planters with shelves and light assemblies.

Elon, Inc.
198 Saw Mill River Road
Elmsford, NY 10523
Imported tile planter kits.

Evergreen Originals
1234 Merchandise Mart
Chicago, IL 60654
Planter packages, complete with plants.

Feathercock, Inc.
2890 West Empire Avenue
P.O. Box 6190
Burbank, CA 91510
Lightweight garden stone for pumice planters.

Fischer Greenhouses
Linwood, NJ 08221
Window planters, lights, terrariums, ferris wheel planters, window shelf planters, many kinds of pots.

Group Artec
P.O. Box 34847
2020 South Robertson Blvd.
Los Angeles, CA 90034
Contemporary design planters sold through designers and decorators.

Heath Manufacturing Co.
Coopersville, MI 49404
Window planters, hanging planters, wishing well planters, hangers, most made from redwood.

The House Plant Corner Ltd.
Box 5000
Cambridge, MD 21613
Pole planters, terrarium kits, planter carts, lights, window planters.

Hyponex Co., Inc.
Copley, OH 44321
Various styles of planters and accessories.

J–Mar Crafts
4840 San Francisco Street
Rocklin, CA 95677
Several different styles of planters.

Kaleidoscope
2201 Faulkner Road, NE
Atlanta, GA 30324
Basket planters, wicker pedestal planters, ceramic gazebo planters.

Lenart Ltd.
2222 Main Street
Evanston, IL 60202
Knocked-down planters, pine plant stands.

Lord and Burnham
Irvington, NY 10533
Window greenhouses. .

London Garden Associates Ltd.
P.O. Box 333
Ridgefield, CT 06877
Grosfillex self-watering planters.

Molded Fiber Glass Tray Co.
East Erie Street
Linesville, PA 16424
Fiber glass flower boxes, zinc-plated steel wall brackets.

Walter F. Nicke
Box 667 G
Hudson, NY 12534
Hanging platforms, pot and saucer holders, strawberry pyramid planters, polypropylene planters.

Paeco, Inc.
500 Market Street
Perth Amboy, NJ 08861
Plant hanging devices.

Quincrafts Corp.
542 East Squantum Street
Quincy, MA 02171
Stained glass planter kits.

Riekes Crisa Corp.
P.O. Box 1271 Downtown
Omaha, NB 68107
Terrarium planters, pottery planters, mirror and glass planters.

Rosenwach, Inc.
40–25 Crescent Street
Long Island City, NY 11101
Redwood planters in many designs.

Skyhook
Route 40
Greenwich, NY 12834
Planter hangers.

Stim-U-Plant
2077 Parkwood Avenue
Columbus, Ohio 43219
Natural look planters.

Swiss Farms Inc.
Philmont, NY 12565
Various styles of plastic planters.

Tube Craft Inc.
1311 West 80th Street
Cleveland, Ohio 44102
Wooden indoor light assemblies, plant stands, redwood flora carts, timers, lights, humidifiers.

Union Products Inc.
P.O. Box 513
Leominster, MA 01453
Hanging planters, kettle planters, patio planters, terrarium planters.

Lillian Vernon
510 South Fulton Avenue
Mt. Vernon, NY 10550
Basket planters, planter saucers, window shelves, pole planters.

Visual Design Manufacturing Co.
6335 Skyline Drive
Houston, TX 77027
Plastic terrarium planters.

Westinghouse Electric Corp.
Westinghouse Building
Gateway Center
Pittsburgh, PA 15222
Indoor lights and stands.

Workbench
470 Park Avenue South
New York, NY 10016
Plastic planters, cube planters.

Yield House
Box 1000
North Conway, NH 03860
Colonial wooden planters, novelty planters.

SEED AND PLANT CATALOGUES/MAIL ORDER ITEMS

Abbey Garden
176 Toro Canyon Road
Carpinteria, CA 93013
Succulents, cacti. Catalogue $1.

Alberts and Merkel Bros., Inc.
2210 South Federal Highway
Boynton Beach, FL 33435
Foliage plants, tropical plants, orchids. 2 lists $1 plus 35¢ handling.

Antonelli Brothers
2545 Capitola Road
Santa Cruz, CA 95062
Tuberous begonias, gloxinias, gladioli, fuchsias. Catalogue free.

Ashwood Specialty Plants
4629 Centinela Avenue
Los Angeles, CA 90066
Unusual succulents, bromeliads, exotic bulbs, ferns, orchids. Catalogue 25¢.

The Bamboo Collection of Robert Lester
280 West 4th Street
New York, NY 10014
Bamboo plants. Price list free.

John Brudy's Rare Plant House
P.O. Box 1348
Cocoa Beach, FL 32931
Seeds, bonsai plants, acacias, palms, banyan trees, exotic plants. Catalogue $1.

Burgess Seed and Plant Co.
Galesburg, MI 49053
Publishes 2 catalogues: Gardening issue with trees, flowers, vegetable seeds; also special Indoor gardening issue devoted to planter gardening. Each $1.

W. Atlee Burpee Co.
Warminster, PA 18974
Strawberry pyramid planters, domed terrarium planters, flower, fruit and vegetable seeds. Catalogue free.

Farmer Seed and Nursery Co.
Faribault, MN 55021
Fruit and vegetable seeds, strawberry climbing tower kits, hanging baskets. Catalogue free.

Fernwood Plants
P.O. Box 268
Topanga, CA 90290
Rare cacti, succulents. List 50¢.

Fischer Greenhouses
Linwood, NJ 08221
African violets. Catalogue 15¢.

Gurney Seed and Nursery Co.
2nd and Capitol
Yankton, SD 57078
Fruit and vegetable seeds, strawberry pyramid planters, gro-lights, plastic planters. Catalogue free.

Joseph Harris Co., Inc.
Moreton Farm
Rochester, NY 14624
Fruit, flower and vegetable seeds, dwarf varieties. Catalogue free.

Hawaiian Flower Exports, Inc.
P.O. Box 249
Mountain View, HA 96771
Anthuriums, dracenas, palms. Catalogue free.

Jerry Horne
10195 S.W. 70th Street
Miami, FL 33173
Rare and unusual plants, aralias, bromeliads, ferns, palms. List, 13¢ self-addressed stamped envelope.

International Growers Exchange
P.O. Box 397
Farmington, MI 48024
Bulbs, house plants, orchids. Catalogue $3.

Le Jardin du Gourmet
Drawer 77
West Danville, VT 05873
Shallots, leeks, herbs, seeds from France, aquamatic planters. Catalogue 25¢.

Jackson and Perkins
Medford, OR 97501
Roses, fruits, flowers, indoor plants, vegetables. Catalogue free.

Jessup's Cactus Nursery
P.O. Box 327
18435 Rea Avenue
Aromas, CA 95004
Cacti. Catalogue free.

Kelly Brothers Nurseries, Inc.
Dansville, NY 14437
Azaleas, flowers, fruits and vegetables, strawberry pyramid planters, bonsai plants. Catalogue free.

Lauray of Salisbury
Undermountain Road
Route 41
Salisbury, CT 06068
Gesneriads, begonias, succulents, fuchsias, cacti. Catalogue 50¢.

Mellinger's
2310 West South Range
North Lima, OH 44452
Hanging baskets, plastic planters, wildflowers, shrubs, trees, rare plants, bonsai planters. Catalogue free.

Merry Gardens
Camden, ME 04843
House plants, hanging basket plants, begonias, fuchsias. Handbook $1.25; list 50¢; both $1.50.

J. E. Miller Nurseries Inc.
Canandaigua, NY 14424
Hanging basket begonias, fruit plants and trees, strawberry pyramid planters. Catalogue free.

Mini-Roses
P.O. Box 4255 Station A
Dallas, TX 75208
Miniature roses, some for hanging baskets. Catalogue 25¢.

Moore Miniature Roses
Sequoia Nursery
2519 East Noble Avenue
Visalia, CA 93277
Miniature roses, some for hanging baskets. Catalogue free.

Nichols Garden Nursery
1190 North Pacific Highway
Albany, OR 97321
Gourmet vegetable seeds, sedums,herb plants and seeds. Catalogue free.

Nuccio's Nurseries
3555 Chaney Trail
Altadena, CA 91001
Rare camellias and azaleas. Price list free.

Orchids by Hausermann, Inc.
P.O. Box 363
Elmhurst, IL 60126
Orchids, information on how to raise them. Catalogue $1.

Paradise Gardens
14 May Street
Whitman, MA
Water plants, pools, liners, complete supplies. Catalogue free.

Geo. W. Park Seed Co., Inc.
P.O. Box 31
Greenwood, SC 29647
Flower, fruit, vegetable seeds, hobby house planters, plant hangers. Catalogue free.

Singers' Growing Things
6385 Enfield Avenue
Reseda, CA 91335
Rare succulents and cycads. Catalogue 50¢.

Spring Hill Nurseries
110 Elm Street
Tipp City, Ohio 45371
Bonsai plants, fruits and vegetables, dwarf fruit trees, house plants. Catalogue free.

Sterns Nurseries
Geneva, OH 14456
Terrarium plants, shrubs, flowers, strawberry barrels, strawberry pyramid planters. Catalogue free.

Stokes Seeds Inc.
Box 548
Buffalo, NY 14240
Vegetables, flowers, fruits, plastic planters, hanging basket liners. Catalogue free.

Sunnybrook Farms Nursery
9448 Mayfield Road
Chesterland, Ohio 44026
Herbs, house plants, cacti, succulents, planter brackets, supplies. Catalogue free.

Three Springs Fisheries
Lilypons, MD 21717
Water lilies, lotus, garden pools, accessories. Catalogue $1.

Wayside Gardens
Hodges, SC 29695
Flowering plants, bulbs, house plants. Catalogue $1.

Weston Nurseries Inc.
East Main Street
Route 135
Hopkinton, MA 01748
Winter-hardy plants, shrubs. Catalogue $2 to readers outside New England.

William Tricker, Inc.
74 Allendale Avenue
Saddle River, NJ 07458
    or
7125 Tanglewood Drive
Independence, OH 44131
Water lilies, lotus, bog plants, plastic tub planters, liners. Catalogue free.

Van Ness Water Gardens
2460 North Euclid Avenue
Upland, CA 91786
Bog plants, water lilies, instructions on water gardening. Catalogue 50¢.

Vermont Bean Seed Co.
Way's Lane
Manchester Center, VT 05255
Pea and bean seeds. Catalogue free.

Index